THE
EVERYTHING®
Public Speaking
Book

Dear Reader,

I've had quite a varied career. Currently, I am a freelance journalist writing primarily about business and I also publish a magazine for dentists. But I have also been a marketing director for a vitamin company and a wildlife refuge, managed half a dozen retail stores, sold classic music subscriptions by phone and membership in a business association in person, managed a holistic medical clinic, and did investor relations for publicly held companies . . . among other things.

What did all these jobs have in common? Public speaking in its broadest definition, which can include sales presentations, giving reports at company meetings, and providing training.

Then there was the rest of my life. Speaking skills have been handy to have, whether I was debating political issues, participating on panels at theological conferences, talking at meetings of fellow fans of J. R. R. Tolkien, or being interviewed by the media (usually about my other book, *The Soul of Your Pet: Evidence for the Survival of Animals after Death*).

The most important lesson I've learned is that no matter how much experience you have, always prepare very well. This book will help you.

Scott S. Smith

THE
EVERYTHING
Series

The handy, accessible books in this series give you all you need to tackle a difficult project, gain a new hobby, or even brush up on something you learned back in school but have since forgotten. You can read cover to cover or just pick out information from the four useful boxes.

 Alerts: Urgent warnings

 Essentials: Quick handy tips

 Facts: Important snippets of information

 Questions: Answers to common problems

When you're done reading, you can finally say you know **EVERYTHING**®!

DIRECTOR OF INNOVATION Paula Munier

EXECUTIVE EDITOR, SERIES BOOKS Brielle K. Matson

MANAGING EDITOR, EVERYTHING SERIES Lisa Laing

ASSOCIATE COPY CHIEF Sheila Zwiebel

ACQUISITIONS EDITOR Lisa Laing

DEVELOPMENT EDITOR Brett Palana-Shanahan

PRODUCTION EDITOR Casey Ebert

Visit the entire Everything® series at *www.everything.com*

THE
EVERYTHING®
PUBLIC
SPEAKING
BOOK

Deliver a winning
presentation every time!

SCOTT S. SMITH

avon, massachusetts

This book is dedicated to my parents, Stan and Carol Smith, who taught me to speak at church not too long after I learned to walk.

Copyright ©2008 by F+W Publications, Inc.
All rights reserved. This book, or parts thereof, may not be reproduced in any form without permission from the publisher; exceptions are made for brief excerpts used in published reviews.

An Everything® Series Book.
Everything® and everything.com® are registered trademarks of F+W Publications, Inc.

Published by Adams Media, an F+W Publications Company
57 Littlefield Street, Avon, MA 02322 U.S.A.
www.adamsmedia.com

ISBN 10: 1-59869-622-X
ISBN 13: 978-1-59869-622-6

Printed in Canada.

J I H G F E D C B A

Library of Congress Cataloging-in-Publication Data
is available from the publisher.

This publication is designed to provide accurate and authoritative information with regard to the subject matter covered. It is sold with the understanding that the publisher is not engaged in rendering legal, accounting, or other professional advice. If legal advice or other expert assistance is required, the services of a competent professional person should be sought.

—From a *Declaration of Principles* jointly adopted by a Committee of the American Bar Association and a Committee of Publishers and Associations

Many of the designations used by manufacturers and sellers to distinguish their products are claimed as trademarks. Where those designations appear in this book and Adams Media was aware of a trademark claim, the designations have been printed with initial capital letters.

This book is available at quantity discounts for bulk purchases.
For information, please call 1-800-289-0963.

Contents

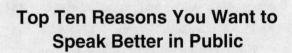

Top Ten Reasons You Want to Speak Better in Public

1. You will never again have to fear being called on to speak.

2. You will be admired as someone who is willing to share valuable information.

3. You will be known as the person who can say something inspiring just when it is needed.

4. You will learn a lot by researching the subjects you talk about.

5. You will do better in business because being articulate is an essential part of being successful.

6. You will meet a lot of interesting new people in your audiences.

7. You will be happier and more confident.

8. You will contribute to making the world a better place.

9. You will have fewer miscommunications with friends, family, and associates.

10. You will come to know yourself much better.

Introduction

The trouble with most books on public speaking is that they have far more information than anyone can readily implement to improve their style. If you read any of these from beginning to end, you realize much of their content is just excessive repetition, slightly differently said, apparently because the writer was required to fill up space. Or the author beats to death a particular angle on the subject. A good deal is also fluff—in terms of knowing what is important about effective public speaking, there is much said that is trivial and that just makes it harder to clearly see what your priorities should be.

This volume gets to the point for each topic, without sacrificing substance. You certainly do not need to apply every technique for reducing nervousness before you speak, but the most effective ones are mentioned (including some "big picture" ideas about self-confidence that are useful to know about beyond the podium).

On the subject of structuring a speech, a lot of fancy theories have been put forth that obscure the fundamentals of communication. You need to just keep your objectives in mind and get others to help you think objectively about how to communicate your message.

When it comes to adding some refinements to the basic outline of your proposed speech, it is good to know how to come up with stories, what quotation sources are best, the process of revising, and the use of repetition. But do not let the desire to seem eloquent get in the way of delivering your message effectively.

A sense of humor is something that every speaker should develop, even if she is not planning to give talks that are meant to be funny. It will serve you well in those awkward moments when the projector does not work, a heckler tries to take over your meeting, or the audience is half asleep.

Likewise, this volume sorts the wheat from the chaff about visual aids. Too many speakers get lazy and try to create the speech around these, rather than using visuals properly for support.

As for becoming skilled at the techniques of argumentation, your planned speech may not be part of a political debate, but the odds are that you will be talking about some topic where there are differing opinions. Whether you are in business or speaking on behalf of a charity, learning how to persuade others to your viewpoint is part of honing your presentation skills.

Few of those who aspire to be regular public speakers have ever been journalists or publicists, so they do not have a hands-on understanding of how the media work. A great deal of grief and even material damage can be avoided if you develop an understanding of the press. And there can be a tremendous upside to your speech or interview if you know how to work with the media.

Finally, for those who are passionate about their favorite topics and feel they have real talent as public speakers, in the last chapters are lessons from professional public speakers about what it takes to succeed in developing demand for your message.

However you use this book, remember to have fun in the process!

Acknowledgments

No man is an island of self-contained, perfect knowledge of everything he needs to write about. I have learned to be a better speaker not only from personal experience, but also from the masters of the art. I especially am indebted to those I consulted for this book, including Jeffrey Jacobi, Howard Shenson, Cliff Atkinson, Harrison Monarth, Larina Kase, Vicki Sullivan, Joanna Slan, James Humes, Susan Drake, and Jeff Davidson, speakers' bureau guru Lilly Walters, comedy writer John Kachuba, as well as media trainers Sally Stewart and T. J. Walker.

And, almost needless to say, you would not be reading this book if it were not for my agent, Robert DiForio of the D4EO Literary Agency, and my editor, Lisa Laing of Adams Media.

A public toast to all of you.

CHAPTER 1

Overcoming Fear

Surveys show that people are more afraid of speaking in public than of dying. In other words, at a funeral they would rather be in the coffin than giving the eulogy! Only about 20 percent of people rarely get nervous when they give a speech and even professional speakers can get butterflies before a major presentation. But no matter what your symptoms might be—the heart pounds, hands go cold, voice quivers—there are many things that can be done to calm down and speak confidently.

The Physiology of Fear

It is okay to be quite anxious before you speak in public. Almost everyone is much of the time. But it is also largely unnecessary, so before you hit the panic button when you are asked to speak, learn about how to manage the symptoms of fear including:

- Heart beating rapidly
- Blushing
- Clammy hands and feet
- Legs and hands trembling
- Rapid breathing and dizziness
- Knotted or queasy stomach
- Sweating
- Dry mouth
- Thin or squeaky voice
- Difficulty concentrating or remembering things

These are the result of the *sympathetic nervous system* pouring adrenaline into the body, preparing it for what is known as the "flight or fight response." When you think you are in danger, the body pumps you up to react. Of course, in the case of giving a speech, you would not be under the threat of dying, you would just be afraid of making an embarrassing mistake in public.

What most people do not realize is that this state of panic will subside naturally in a short time. When fear injects adrenaline, the *parasympathetic nervous system* compensates and calms the body down. The time it takes to return to normal depends on the severity of the reaction and, fortunately, you have the ability to regulate that. Once you get into the speech and take your mind off your fears, the symptoms will subside gradually anyway.

E ssential

Try to recall a time when you received bad news or were really upset. If someone was trying to talk to you at the same time about another matter, it would be hard to concentrate on his words. You could not think clearly. That is a similar mind-body reaction to worrying about speaking in public. The body gears up for a threat the mind perceives and the ability to think is overwhelmed.

It is clear that fears about public speaking are simply the result of thinking distorted by biochemistry. Truly, as President Franklin D. Roosevelt said about a much more serious situation than going up to a podium, "The only thing we have to fear is fear itself—nameless, unreasoning, unjustified terror which paralyzes needed efforts to convert retreat into advance."

Some people are also physiologically wired for shyness. Others may have grown up in a family where speaking up was not encouraged, and they have not had jobs that required verbal facility. Either way, while these add to the challenge of learning to give speeches, any psychological, social, or biological influences can be offset by applying the right techniques.

 **Alert**

The temptation for some people who face a speaking engagement is to relax by having a drink of alcohol. Others resort to taking beta-blocker drugs, which are designed to block adrenaline for patients with heart problems. Either way, you are likely to become too relaxed to do a good job of delivering your speech (not to mention the other risks).

Before you get into specific exercises to offset the symptoms of stage fright, first consider how you can make your body more speech-ready. It may seem like a tangent if you think successful speechmaking is a color-by-numbers process, just a matter of learning some tricks. You can discover for yourself why starting with physical and psychological preparedness makes more sense.

The Foundation of a Holistic Approach

It should be obvious that the body affects the functioning of the brain and, therefore, the mind. How well you take care of your health can also determine how calm you remain in stressful situations and how much energy you can muster to give an enthusiastic presentation. Treat yourself like an athlete in training and you will help yourself win the game of public speaking. A holistic approach means using every possible means to provide the best result for mind and body.

Fuel for Stamina and Health

Would you put a bad grade of gasoline in your car on purpose? Judging by the sales of junk food and the dramatic increase in obesity, few Americans understand much about what fuel to put into their bodies. Doctors are often not equipped to guide their patients because they barely study nutrition in medical school. Take responsibility and learn the basics about nutrition so that you can improve the odds of staying healthy.

E ssential

Do not eat a big, fat-rich meal the day you are making a speech or else your body's need to put energy into the digestive process will slow down your mind. Try a light meal, like fruit or salad, a few hours before. Do not try to give yourself a boost by drinking coffee—you will speak too fast and need a bathroom break!

Robert Haas's *Eat to Win in the 21st Century* is a sensible, balanced source of information on why to add more complex carbohydrates (whole grains, nuts, legumes, beans, fruits, and vegetables) to your diet. As important as adding more fiber and nutrients is excluding the three whites: white sugar, white flour, and white rice. They all are used by the body in a way that causes your blood sugar to gyrate. When blood sugar is low, so will be your energy level, you will become confused, and your mood will go up and down. There are substitutes that taste just as good and are healthier. With modest changes in diet, a good multivitamin-mineral supplement (calcium, magnesium, and B vitamins help keep the body calm), and plenty of pure water, you will be astounded at how much better you will feel, how much physical energy you can bring to bear for a speech, and how clearly you will be able to think. You will also be less likely to be sick when the big day to speak arrives.

Regular Exercise

A lot of books about public speaking stress particular exercises that can be done to help lower anxiety (which will be discussed in a moment). What is generally not mentioned, though, is that regular exercise will lower your overall anxiety level, making you less susceptible to the biological aspects of fear of failure in public. If you have experienced the "runner's high," then you have some appreciation for the mind-body relationship. If you do not already have an exercise program, start doing some modest exercise for at least thirty minutes three times a week: get on a treadmill, go to the gym to lift weights, run, or do some fast walking. Swimming can be especially good for improving whole-body conditioning and to help the body to relax afterward.

Adequate Rest

Getting enough rest is clearly important to being able to speak in a vigorous style. Nothing will bore the audience quicker than someone who is too exhausted to speak with enthusiasm, no matter how well a speech is written and how much practicing has been done. Studies show that most people need eight hours of sleep every day to be at their physical and mental peak. You may not think so because you are in such a constant state of tension and so revved up by caffeine that you believe you are doing fine. If you have a hard time falling or staying asleep, try different kinds of over-the-counter medications or herbal remedies. If these do not work for you, consult a doctor.

If you can take a fifteen- to twenty-minute nap in the afternoon— or even just close your eyes and relax in a chair somewhere quiet— you will definitely feel invigorated.

Take Care of Your Voice

It should go without saying that if you smoke, you need to quit if you want to be a regular speaker. Smoking can leave you breathless at inappropriate times, not to mention making you vulnerable to horrible hacking coughs magnified by the microphone. A smoker's voice is also not considered pleasant to listen to by most people. You should even avoid being in smoky environments right before a speech.

It should also be obvious that you do not want to scream at a sports event or otherwise abuse your vocal cords in the days before a speech. If you need to talk a lot, do it in a moderate tone to avoid strain. Also, make sure you have adequate humidity at home to avoid getting a dry throat.

Calm Winds from the East

The calmer and more centered you are, the better speaker you can be because you will have better control of all your faculties. And you certainly will be less bothered by the passing symptoms of the fear of giving speeches. Following are a few more advanced techniques from Asian cultures that can help you stay physically calm before a speaking engagement (and there is no need to even know about the spiritual theories behind them).

Martial Arts

Some five million Americans practice a form of martial arts (not counting those enrolled in kickboxing, Tae Bo, and other aerobic spin-offs at gyms). Although there are styles that come from elsewhere in the world (including Israel and Brazil), the East Asian schools emphasize mental and spiritual preparation as much as physical training. Balancing the *chi*, or the body's energy flow, is considered essential, just as it is in acupuncture and other forms of traditional Asian medicine.

 Fact

Karate and tae kwon do are famous for using fast hand and foot thrusts for self-defense. Wing Chun kung fu is the only style created by a woman and is especially suited for those who have a small frame (this was martial arts star Bruce Lee's specialty). Tai chi is known for its graceful, dance-like movements.

All martial arts require dedication to master, but practitioners extol the results, including a feeling of centeredness and increased control over body and mind. And few health practices can instill the self-confidence that learning a martial art can, something that will improve your ability to talk from the podium.

Meditation

Transcendental Meditation, or TM, one of many schools of meditation, became popular in the United States starting in the 1960s. Today, its advocates point to 600 studies they say have provided scientific support that, among many other claims, TM decreases anxiety, lowers blood pressure, and improves memory and sleep. TM advocates advise spending twenty minutes twice a day sitting in a comfortable position, focused on a word in the Sanskrit language (known as a mantra), which helps keep the mind clear and calm. At the same time, putting awareness on taking and releasing slow breaths helps to keep the mind from being distracted by trivial thoughts.

 Alert

Meditation is best undertaken with the guidance of an experienced and reputable teacher. Some people who spend an excessive amount of time doing meditation can undergo psychological and physiological problems, including disorientation, experiencing upsetting emotions, and physical discomfort.

Other methods of meditation involve visualization of an image or contemplation of a spiritual truth, but the general effects are the same.

Yoga

Increasingly popular in the United States, yoga is a series of postures, breathing exercises, and movements that originated in India as spiritual practices (to revitalize psychic energy networks). There are different systems, all of which relieve tension and stress and improve flexibility, muscle tone, and stamina. Research has shown that yoga can also give a boost to the immune system and alleviate a long list of health problems, from arthritis to heart disease. Concentration, creativity, and self-esteem are also said to improve.

Exercises Before the Speech

A couple of hours before you go to the podium, you can do some general, mild exercises in a gym or in your room or go for a brisk, brief walk to reduce nervous energy.

There are also some specific exercises that will alleviate the symptoms of stage fright that can be practiced right before you go on. Actually, it is helpful for your long-term physical and mental conditioning if you practice some of these regularly, rather than waiting for the crisis of a speaking engagement.

 **Question**

How can I fix a voice that becomes squeaky under stress?
Tape-record part of your speech and practice keeping your normal tone in a range that sounds calm and collected. It also helps not to stress your vocal cords in the days before a speech. Putting on lip balm, chewing gum to stimulate saliva production right before you go on, and then sips of water at the podium (not too much) will keep the whole vocal apparatus in shape.

Deep breathing can be a stress reliever or actually have the opposite effect. When you panic you may suddenly start breathing rapidly, either deeply or shallowly. The key to calming down is to take a deep inhaling breath that expands the stomach, not the chest, over a four-second period. Then hold it for the same amount of time, exhale for another four seconds, and finally, wait four seconds before inhaling again. A few minutes of doing this and you should feel relaxed.

Stretching helps, too. Open your mouth as wide as possible, let your jaw just hang for a bit, and then take a deep yawn. Roll your head around 360 degrees a few times and then reverse the direction. Slump forward and let your arms hang, like a rag doll, shake yourself, and then stand tall and swing your arms from side to side. Stretch your arms as high as you can and stand on your toes.

Tightening each muscle in your body for a few seconds and then completely relaxing it has a tension-dissipating effect similar to using weights at the gym. You can start at your feet and move up to your face. For the shoulders, do some shrugs; for the chest, tighten the muscles of the armpits; for the back, first jut out your chest, then drop your head down. You will probably be surprised at how tense you are when you start—and how relaxed you feel just before you are going to speak.

Other Methods

If you have trouble exercising enough to get relaxed in time, whether there are physical or time constraints, there are two other techniques that may compensate.

Massage

Massage may be the oldest form of medical care and is shown in 5,000-year-old Egyptian tomb paintings. Getting a massage on a regular basis from a licensed professional is a good way to force yourself to relax, but even getting a shoulder massage from a friend right before you go on stage can help.

Primal Scream

If nothing else dissipates the tension, consider exercising your lungs. Go where no one is likely to hear you—like a stairwell or by the trash in the back of a building—and just let out a full-throated scream as long as you can. You can do it more than once, if you feel the need, and you should feel better afterward (as long as no one calls the police!).

Once you have used various types of exercise to put your body in a more relaxed state most of the time and know what to do right before you speak, you can turn to psychological techniques that will also help.

CHAPTER 2

The Psychology of Fear

Fear is both a physiological challenge and a psychological one. Anything competitive—like sports events, war, or being compared by an audience with other speakers they have already heard—inspires the mobilization of personal resources to succeed. While you are working to improve your physical resilience, you need to also turn to the arena of psychology, emotions, practice, and delivery to build your skills. The more self-confidence you have, the less fear you are likely to experience at the podium.

Know Your Audience

The best way to avoid a nervous meltdown on stage is to know your topic and what people in the audience need to hear. That starts with as much research as you have time to do.

Every speech should be constructed with the particular audience that will be addressed in mind. The Internet has made doing research on any subject easier than ever, although it does require some time to sort through the choices. Punch in "Indianapolis marketing demographics" and you will get 420,000 hits to consider. The local chamber of commerce, the club president, the teacher of the class, the rabbi who will be introducing you, or the union steward who asked you to speak can give you useful background. Industry publications, city magazines and newspapers, local tourism and business Web sites, and even those who have spoken to the same group before can also be helpful resources.

Ask about age, politics, religion, education level, and diversity of professions of those likely to attend, as well as revered cultural and sports institutions and historical highlights of the group or city. Determine if there are sensitive issues within your topic for this group and how well the average attendee is likely to understand the basics.

**Alert**

When you are at the podium, do not mistake blank faces for apathy or hostility. Some people do not smile when they are concentrating on what is being said. Others may be simply withholding judgment until they hear more. And remember that your impressions are distorted under the influence of adrenaline. There is no reason to be paranoid.

Getting to the hall early will allow you to meet some attendees and get a sense of who they are and why they are there. This will bring that scary crowd down to individual human beings, help you connect with the group emotionally, and tell you something about what to say—or not.

Master Your Material

The best way to instill self-confidence is to know more about your subject than your audience does. That is usually pretty easy because people would not come to listen to you if they thought they already knew everything about the topic. To avoid overconfidence in your thesis, make sure you look at your sources with some degree of skepticism. Read books and articles with opposing viewpoints and anticipate questions challenging the conclusions you present. But while you are researching, only make notes on the important points—do not get lost in studying too much trivia that will clutter your mind.

Give Yourself Time to Write

It should go without saying that you need to spend as much time as possible working on the logical organization of your remarks. Before you agree to speak, determine how much free time you will have before the date, then how long you believe you will need to research and write your talk (and remember to pad the estimate to include worst-case scenarios, such as illness or a deadline at work that is moved up). If you discipline yourself to get this done well in advance, you will be less likely to be nervous.

 Fact

As Harrison Monarth and Larina Kase explain in *The Confident Speaker*, it is human nature to want to avoid stress-inducing situations like public speaking, but this actually makes the problem worse because it never allows you to improve. When forced to speak, "avoiders" overcompensate by rushing through the speech or overrehearsing until the presentation is too mechanical. Approach each speaking opportunity as a chance to make an incremental improvement.

Practice Makes Good Enough

Ideally, you would either be making the speech with presentation slides, cue cards, or a copy that has been highlighted. Talks that are read verbatim sound less sincere. People may think that someone else could have written your remarks and that maybe you are not really an expert. It is also hard to establish an emotional connection with the audience when you are reading. So practice using key word notes or an outline, but have your full speech on the podium, too. If you panic and cannot remember the material with just notes, read the speech. In that event, read a couple of sentences to yourself and then look up as you say them before returning to the page. This will help you connect with people rather than just staring at your manuscript.

Videotape at least one rehearsal and watch it to learn how to improve (or audiotape it, which will help you eliminate filler expressions like "um" and "uh"). Try to get a few friends to listen to see how you do in front of real people rather than empty chairs (but insist on candid feedback or they will likely be too polite). If you trip over phrases, simplify the wording. Memorize the opening and closing paragraphs of the speech, to be sure you start and end with your best foot forward.

What you need to achieve is not perfection. People in the audience are not interested in whether you deliver the speech 100 percent as you wrote and practiced it: they just want you to get out of the way of your message.

Improve Your Enunciation

Most people are unaware of how difficult it may be for those from other areas of the United States or from other countries (who have been trained in "standard English") to understand their accent or dialect. In some regions, dropping final consonants (find becomes fine in the South) or changing pronunciation from the norm (Cuba becomes Cuber in Boston) would be acceptable for a speaker from that area addressing a local audience. A speech coach can help you become aware of challenges to being understood outside your home base. But even without professional help, if you strive to clearly enunciate your words with a strong voice, it will add another factor to the success of your presentation.

Alert

Do not do your last practice run right before going to bed the night before the speech. That would stimulate your mind too much and keep you up, just when a good night's sleep is critical.

An excellent do-it-yourself course on minimizing distracting aspects of a regional accent and improving enunciation is on the CD that accompanies Jeffrey Jacobi's *How to Say It with Your Voice.*

Dress for Success

Think carefully about what you need to wear. The audience may consist of doctors at a resort in Hawaii who are dressed in shorts, which would not be appropriate for you. That does not mean you have to be formal—it may be fine for male speakers to just wear slacks and a blazer without a tie and women may be comfortable speaking in a business pantsuit. The only rule, besides being clean and neat, is that your appearance should convey your personality and your authoritativeness. Check clothes and makeup in a mirror fifteen minutes before you go on.

Women should wear low to medium heels. High heels will be uncomfortable to stand in for the duration of the speech, and they could result in falling on stage. Men should be sure their shoes do not squeak.

Get to the Hall Early

Travel earlier than you "need" to, in case there are flight or traffic problems. When you arrive at the hall, do a sound check to see how close you should be to the microphone (do not hold one, if you think your hand may shake). If you will have to use a lapel (lavalier) mike, practice walking around the stage and returning to the podium as you need to look at your notes. Make sure any equipment you need to use actually works (always have an emergency kit of spare items you may need, as well as a backup plan if that is not enough). Practice getting on and off the stage without tripping. Make sure there is a glass or bottle of water at the podium (not cold, as that will freeze up your vocal cords). Determine if the air conditioning or heating is at a comfortable level for as many people as are expected in the room (better that it is a little cool, since people get drowsy when too warm).

And most important, carry a spare copy of your speech in a pocket, in case your luggage or briefcase gets lost.

E ssential

Be careful when you select jewelry to wear on stage. Bracelets that jangle, earrings that dazzle, and necklaces that are ostentatious can turn listeners into viewers who are not paying attention to your presentation.

Out-Psych the Fear

An upgrade of your health and energy, exercise, and proper preparation will help keep you calm when you get on stage. But you may want to go beyond these basics to be sure the fear is under control.

This Is Your Crusade

You are considered an expert on the subject you are going to be speaking about or you would not have been invited to take up the audience's time listening to you. That should mean that you are passionate about the topic and that you have devoted a good part of your life to mastering the details. Here is a perhaps rare opportunity where everyone will be waiting on your every word. You should feel excited in a good way!

Visualization

Many top athletes prepare for competitions mentally by visualizing themselves winning. Right before he hits the ball, Tiger Woods imagines the flight path it will take, watching a movie in his mind. Also known as guided imagery, this process of using the mind's eye to marshal all the powers of the brain and body can be a powerful aid in achieving goals. Classic handbooks on the process, like Shakti

Gawain's *Creative Visualization* and William Fezler's *Creative Imagery*, stress the importance of developing vivid sensory recall of the details of what a successful action would look and feel like.

The subconscious (the part of your mind that is outside your conscious awareness) is especially able to align thinking and actions in the right direction when the brain is giving off alpha waves. That is when you are very relaxed, such as just before you fall asleep or wake up. Take time to relax each muscle progressively before you start imagining the outcome of your speech.

 Fact

> The process of visualization has been successfully used by therapists to treat skin diseases, obesity, phobias, sexual dysfunction, alcoholism, depression, asthma, gastrointestinal troubles, anxiety, insomnia, speech problems, and other medical and behavioral dysfunctions. It is a natural way to combat stage fright.

Affirmations

Positive self-talk has become popular in recent years as a way of stopping the negative chatter of the dysfunctional mind. In *The Life We Are Given*, Michael Murphy and George Leonard of Esalen Institute, the pioneering personal transformation center in Big Sur, California, suggest guidelines based on extensive experience for making these affirmations more powerful.

They advise using the present tense in formulating them: "I am calm as I speak in public," instead of "I will be calm." They explain that this turns it into "an instrument for creating a parallel, present-tense reality in your consciousness." They believe that you should use only three primary affirmations in any one period, about all the mind can handle effectively at one time. But also add one that says, "My entire being is balanced, vital, and healthy." This will check the tendency of the subconscious to trip you up by misinterpreting words in the other three.

There are several ways to integrate these affirmations into your life. You can relax and repeat the phrases in your mind, or they can be chanted. Affirmations can also be combined with meditation and visualization. You can also write down the affirmations each day and carry the messages with you to look at periodically (when you feel fear about your speech, for example).

Get to the Root of Fear

There are several techniques for mastering unnecessary fear of public speaking that are significantly more effective at getting at the roots of the fear.

Hypnotherapy

Rituals to induce a trance have been recorded since the beginning of history, often in conjunction with religious mysteries. In 1842, Scottish neurosurgeon James Braid wrote a booklet identifying hypnotism as "the induction of a habit of intense concentration of attention" to the extent that breathing became slow and shallow.

Hypnotherapy, the use of the hypnotic state to treat a physical or mental condition, is perhaps the most underutilized miracle tool in medicine (stage hypnotists use the same state for entertainment purposes). There are numerous scientific studies that validate the use of hypnosis for anxiety, stress, smoking addiction, insomnia, pain management, headaches, and other disorders. The most effective way to use a hypnosis session to achieve a goal is to tape-record it and then listen to the tape as you fall asleep for twenty-one nights. This will help embed the message in the subconscious.

Psychotherapy

If you feel extremely shy about getting on stage and instructing others, you might want to consider the unique help available from psychotherapy. Few Americans have had the experience because it has had a stigma that the only people who need it are "in trouble" or "crazy." While it is true that people often see a psychologist or a psychiatrist when they face disturbing problems in their lives, patients do tend to be both wealthier and more educated than average. After achieving some level of material success people facing serious difficulties in their professional or personal lives may seek the benefits of therapy. Far from being a technique to fix "nut cases," it is actually a very sophisticated way to get to know yourself. This may seem paradoxical to those with low self-esteem, but as you come to know yourself better, you will have more self-confidence about expressing yourself in public.

 Fact

Sigmund Freud, who founded the school of psychoanalysis, started out as a hypnotherapist in the 1890s, but believed his "talking cure" was more effective and by 1905 had abandoned overtly using hypnosis. But in 1919, he decided that combining the two could speed the recovery of his patients.

There are numerous schools of therapy that are based on theories about how the mind works and the best way to heal dysfunction, as described in *The Everything® Psychology Book* by Lesley Bolton. Many use dream interpretation to bring to conscious awareness the wishes of the subconscious. Free-form association of words is another way to get around conscious defense mechanisms. A structured talking-out of a problem is always helpful in becoming more objective about it; studies show that putting feelings into words has a calming effect. Cognitive behavioral therapy is one school that has become popular as a way of achieving change quicker than traditional methods. It emphasizes identifying errors of thought, such as overgeneralization and magnification of negatives.

Using psychotherapeutic drugs has also become another way to gain some of the benefits, such as relief from depression, in a relatively fast and less expensive way. However, they do not completely substitute for psychotherapy.

E ssential

Regardless of whether any other technique works, a good way to distract yourself from worrying about speaking is to engage in some fun the night before. Go dancing, watch a movie, see a show, or immerse yourself in conversation with friends over dinner.

Spiritual Support

A spiritual path, defined in the broadest terms as belief that there is more to life than the material world, can help you work through the challenges of becoming a successful speaker.

In the famous twelve-step programs used to treat addictions, the individual is asked to turn himself over to the will of a Higher Power. While most people would call this God, these programs stress that it is possible for an agnostic or even an atheist to succeed by seeing the support group in this role as "a power greater than yourself." Or one could believe that miracles come about through the mysterious powers of the mind. You might pray for success in achieving the goals of your speech and that you will be inspired to say the right things in the best way.

There are a number of programs that address the psychological and spiritual "big picture" issues that enhance emotional stability, such as the Landmark Forum, InnerQuest Adventures, Tony Robbins's personal transformation seminars, and The Artist's Way workshops (based on the book of the same name by Julia Cameron, these involve exercises to enhance creativity).

At the Podium

Your body language during the speech will project nervousness or confidence. Stand straight, do not grip the lectern as if it is the only thing holding you up, and do not shift back and forth on your legs too much—stand comfortably balanced. If your hands are trembling, do not hold any paper when you speak. Be aware of fidgeting, jangling the keys in your pocket, brushing your hair, adjusting your glasses, or other nervous habits. If sweat appears on your face, just dab at it with a folded handkerchief. Do not look at the back wall to avoid stares— just shift your eyes every couple of sentences to someone new and smile at each person. Speak clearly and with enthusiasm.

 Fact

The truth is that speakers assume the audience will notice nervousness more than most members actually will. Speakers are projecting their feelings onto the audience, which is generally unaware there is any problem.

And if you feel nervous energy, know that it can be channeled to convey enthusiasm, so be grateful to ride that wave. Your audience will be less likely to be bored.

One manifestation of nerves is the tendency to exaggerate the odds of failure and the consequences. But what really will happen if you just cannot tamp down all the symptoms of nervousness? If you stumble over your words and appear a little shaky, this may actually make you seem more sympathetic to the audience—you would appear humble, sincere, and not too slick.

And what is the real likelihood of 100 percent failure? Probably zero. Maybe you will not completely persuade a majority of the people to your point of view, but the odds are you will at least inform most and influence some.

 **Alert**

Do not bother trying to keep calm by imagining your audience naked or on the toilet. Although they have had their advocates (including Winston Churchill and Carol Burnett), these techniques are usually not effective and could be distracting.

The worst-case scenarios are not so bad after all. As feminist leader Gloria Steinem, who has suffered stage fright all her life, commented: "There is no right way to speak, only your way; you don't die; and it's worth it."

CHAPTER 3

The Informative Speech

B efore you begin to write your speech, consider your objective. Is it primarily to persuade the audience to believe in or do something? Are you supposed to keep the audience laughing? Do you just want to educate them about an interesting topic? To some extent, these categories of persuasion, entertainment, and information sharing overlap, since you want to use elements of each to maximize the effect of your talk. This chapter will focus on the substance of all speeches: how to present facts in a way that will help the audience understand their meaning and remember what you said.

Information Please!

Much has been made of different kinds of speeches. Two of these, the persuasive and the entertaining speeches, require quite a bit of specialized effort. In order to deliver a speech of persuasion, you have to develop lawyerly skills of argumentation, whether or not you are sharing the podium with someone representing an opposing view (see Chapter 9). To be able to deliver a primarily entertaining speech, you would want to develop a strong sense of humor (see Chapter 6).

But most speeches need to inform the audience to one degree or another. To convince people of your point of view, you need to provide background to the issues. For the audience to appreciate a joke at a roast, it needs to be reminded of the joke's basis in the characteristics of the person being celebrated. So let's take a closer look at informative or informational speeches as a model for creating any kind of presentation. Examples include:

- Training employees to use a new software program
- Reporting on a comparison of competitive products to the sales force
- Teaching a Sunday school class about the life of St. Paul
- Giving an oral report about the French Revolution in a college class
- Providing an eyewitness account in court
- Giving the toast at a wedding
- Being interviewed on TV
- Delivering a financial status report to the board of directors of a nonprofit organization
- Presenting an award to someone at an industry convention
- Teaching a class on how to invest
- Offering the eulogy at a funeral

Almost everyone will have the occasion to need the ability to deliver informative speeches, no matter how short. If you are selected to give a presentation, it will probably be because people believed you would provide a fair and thorough account of the subject within the time limit. Remind yourself of that when you pick and choose among the available facts and information on your topic.

Research the Topic

When you are deciding whether to accept an invitation to speak, be sure you have enough time to do sufficient research, especially if you have only a superficial grasp of the subject. Even if you are considered an expert, you may find that new discoveries, events, and analyses by other scholars have changed the quantity of information that needs to be reviewed. You also need to take into consideration the level of education about the issues that members of the audience have. If you are giving a ten-minute report on the history of the federal electoral college for the Women's Club, the amount of detail you will need to convey will be very different from what you will want to know to make a half-hour presentation at a political science class.

E ssential

Specialists in a topic may have a narrow and biased viewpoint, but you want to listen to what they say because a strong opinion can lead to an analysis that would otherwise be overlooked. Just be aware of the difference between relatively unbiased reference material and scholarly opinions and note who seems to make the best arguments and where they disagree.

The reference desk at a library can be invaluable to find reliable information in the print world. The Internet, wonderful though it is, is a virtual haystack that is difficult to search through to find anything useful at times. Books do not get into print without rigorous checking by authors and editors, in order to avoid factual errors and unintentional plagiarism. Reference librarians have lots of experience to know where to confirm obscure facts, find helpful statistics, or pin down a quote you cannot find through your own efforts. Libraries carry many volumes that are not online, are only available by subscription or at a price you do not want to pay, or that are out of print and not available to buy even from the largest used-book sources. The industry reference section of any library can be especially useful.

Make notes about both the content and the source when you research, whether online or off, so that if your assertion is challenged or you want to look up the source again, you will know where to go. Use 3 x 5 cards for each group of related facts from one source, then put them into alphabetical order by name of volume or site. Be sure you have a sense of priority about the information you collect—

almost as bad as doing too little research is doing so much that you become lost in a sea of facts that you cannot readily organize.

 Fact

As a supplement to the world of ink and librarians, the Virtual Reference Desk at *www.refdesk.com* is a gold mine. It groups helpful links together, such as over 5,000 U.S. and overseas news sources that range from the *Taipei Times* to the Islamic Republic News Agency.

Structure Your Speech

Speeches have three parts: introduction, body, and conclusion. The body can be written first and the opening and closing can be fit around it afterward. It is often said that the initial and final paragraphs of a speech are the most important and you need to sweat over them: you retain the audience's attention or lose it with the opening, and the closing will be what they remember most. This is a half-truth—these are the most important parts, but they are also the easiest to work out. There are a hundred clever ways to open and close any presentation, so anyone who fails has not made the right choices or did not do a good job on the delivery. The real challenge is the main body of the talk: you need to provide enough regular stimulation to keep the audience engaged or the only thing members will remember is ". . . and I appreciated your invitation to speak to you today."

Grand Opening

Whether you jump up and down and scream "I love Elvis" or sing a moving song for your opening, there are really no rules about how to start a speech. Only one thing is certain: everyone will be paying attention for those few moments. You also want to be sure you have this part learned so well (not necessarily memorized word for word) that you do not have to look at notes. Following are some time-tested winning approaches.

E ssential

"Lucidity of speech is unquestionably one of the surest tests of mental precision . . . In my experience a confused talker is never a clear thinker"—David Lloyd George, Prime Minister of the United Kingdom, 1916-1922.

Humor

Some books on introductions for speeches advise not telling jokes: if you fail, the audience will tune out, they warn. Poppycock: a humorous opening is often the best way to endear yourself to an audience, providing it is relevant to your topic (if it is just tacked on, it will have the opposite effect). As explained in Chapter 6, there are endless sources for jokes that can be customized to the occasion. But you do need to memorize the basic elements of the joke, if not the precise wording, decide what to emphasize and where to pause, and then rehearse it until you always get a laugh from your practice audience. Select well and practice well and there is no need to avoid humor right out of the gate.

Quotation

Unless a quote is extraordinarily perceptive, it is always wisest to quote someone or something well known to the particular audience for your opening. The two most obvious sources (because familiarity often means wide acceptance of the sense behind the thought) would be the Bible (taking up forty-six pages in *Bartlett's Familiar*

Quotations) and Shakespeare (fifty-three pages). However, if the more apt quote comes from an obscure source, just explain in one line who or what it was. If the source is anonymous, that is less desirable, but it does not really matter, as long as the comment is insightful. A surprising source—former Republican presidential candidate Barry Goldwater condoning gay marriage or a rancher who is a vegetarian—will catch extra attention. For more ideas, see the quotation section of Chapter 4.

Anecdote

The popularity of storytelling is evidenced in the public's thirst for movies. An anecdote to illustrate the theme of your talk taps into this for a perfect start. The mind remembers a story even better than a joke because a picture of someone doing something is more easily visualized. If it is a personal experience that underscores your knowledge of the subject, all the better. If the story has some dialogue, you could have fun mimicking the parties (no one will expect you to be a pro, it just makes your opener more attention-getting). For more tips on storytelling, see Chapter 4.

Rhetorical Question

Why is voter turnout so low? Why are felons let out of prisons early? If you start with a sharp question, you are not necessarily asking for a show of hands: you are engaging the minds of the audience members to be curious about the answer you are about to provide.

 **Alert**

It is fine to start by thanking your host for the opportunity to speak, but do not give a complete laundry list of everyone on the dais or it will put the audience to sleep as quickly as an Oscar acceptance speech. Move on to your real opening to grab their attention.

Surprising Statistic

The Los Angeles high school graduation rate is only 44 percent and New York City's is 39 percent. Around 100,000 people die each year because of mistakes in treatment made in U.S. hospitals. A startling statistic will get the crowd to sit up and pay attention.

A Local Reference

Audiences like visiting speakers who are not delivering the same canned speech everywhere, but rather show personal interest in the local culture. Start by making a reference to a sports rivalry, the work habits of the mayor, the extreme weather, an anniversary of importance, a local hero.

Common Ground

Talk about how you share the values of the audience: their passion for the second amendment's guarantee of the right to bear arms, your appreciation for the charity activities of the Elks, the fact that you grew up nearby. The transition to the body of the speech then ties together the opening remarks with the relevance to the main theme. "Now that you know I care deeply about these issues, let me tell you some of the conclusions I've drawn after years of study and experience in this field."

Strategy for the Body

There are many ways you can approach how to lay out the information so that the audience can readily understand it and the relationships of the parts to the whole. Without an obvious pattern to give context, people have a difficult time absorbing and retaining information that fits into a bigger picture of why they should care about it.

Alphabetical

If you want to discuss a series of things that do not lend themselves to some other logical sequence, you could talk about them in alphabetical order, such as cities with low crime or the frequency of family names in a state (or this sequence of strategies).

Cause and Effect

Illuminating the real causes that led to certain results may help your audience to grasp a meaningful relationship better than a simple chronology. You might be discussing a scholarly analysis of the role of protection of slavery versus states rights as motivators for the formation of the Confederacy. Or you could be explaining the results of a failed marketing plan.

Chronology

If the order of occurrence is of primary concern, however, a chronology may be ideal. You could be recounting the origins, highlights, and future prospects for the Israeli-Palestinian peace process. The evolution of a new toothpaste might have a very short but detail-rich history, with implications for developing other products.

E *ssential*

It is often asserted that people do not retain more than three big points from a presentation. Of course, the reality varies widely: someone who is half-asleep after lunch may not remember anything, while someone else on the front row who thinks you are making fundamental errors in assumption will hang on every word. Keeping the structure of the speech simple and uncluttered with unnecessary facts will help retention.

Complexity or Difficulty

You may want to start with a discussion of simple systems and gradually move to more complex ones or easy versus difficult challenges. Examples could be comparing the characteristics of 1950s television sets with today's high-definition TVs, or the difficulties facing a group that are easily solved and then the intractable problems.

Geographic or Spatial

You could arrange the discussion in terms of spatial relationships or location. For example, you are giving a status report on the construction of a building and present this floor by floor. Or you are discussing the future of church missionary work by continent.

Letter Sequence

One memory trick to help people retain the message is to assign meaning to each letter in a word: LOVE can stand for Losing Our Valuable Earth or Letting Others View Everything.

Extended Analogy or Metaphor

Analogy helps to explain something by comparison with something else that has some similarities: relating the fourth quarter of a football game to your company's fourth quarter results. Metaphors are a subset of analogies that make more complex and whole identifications. An extended metaphor would be to relate the story of King Arthur as a struggle between a wise old order against the dangers of brash upstarts.

Numerical Order

If you were examining different parts of a whole, it could help the audience pay attention to the entire list if you number them: three competing economic theories, or your summary of an article that is going to be in six bite-size pieces. Tell them how many points you will be covering before you start.

Problem and Solution

If you are addressing a group to provide your expertise to solve a problem, you need to first assess the awareness of the audience. If some members know almost nothing, you can at least briefly review how the challenge developed until the crisis point, and then present different ways to resolve it in more detail. Your Masonic lodge may have dwindling membership, or there is not currently enough money to provide adequate marketing for the symphony's program this year.

Trends

You could present information in terms of significant meaning in the changes in incidences: a population explosion in Africa or rising sales. This would be a good time to show a chart or slide to help the audience visualize the trend.

Type

In a talk about new video games or this year's winners of art prizes, you could present them in related groups: war games would be reviewed together; first, second, and third prizes in oil would be separated from awards for watercolor.

Once you have laid out a logical presentation of the basic facts, you want to take a few minutes to wrap up.

The Grand Finale

Somehow, you have managed to retain the attention of the audience through the body of the speech without too many falling asleep. Perhaps it was the dramatic rise and fall of your voice, the hilarious asides, the amazing statistics, or striking slides (not to mention the jumping jacks you had everyone do at the halfway point). Finally comes the second-easiest and second-most important part of the talk. Clearly, this is not a time to wing it. You want to announce, as with trumpets, when you are coming down to the wire: even those whose minds have been wandering will tend to perk up, hoping you will say something they can take away with minimal effort. "I would like to make one last point," or "now that our time together has come to a close, let me leave you with this important thought" will alert them to this moment. In addition to the methods you used to create initial interest, remember the following tips.

Summarize

Tell them what you told them. If you were one of several speakers, this is especially important to help you stand out from all the things that have been said that day. Reiterate your main points.

 **Alert**

> Never go over your allotted speaking time. If you practice carefully without rushing, you should finish a few minutes early, allowing time for starting late, interruptions, and audience laughter. If you are asked to finish a little early, be prepared to cut secondary points and keep to your planned closing.

Use Strong Language

Close with eloquent power phrases like "moving forward to meet the future" or "let us all get up tomorrow, determined to overcome this evil together." Action words, vivid imagery, and alliteration (the repetition of similar sounds) will create a strong closing.

Remind Them You Are Right

If you have not only informed them, but drawn conclusions you want them to share, use forceful, positive language. "As we have seen tonight, no informed student of UFOs can dismiss them as swamp gas or the planet Venus" or "Clearly, conventional wisdom in Western medicine about acupuncture has been far behind the evidence."

An Emotional Appeal

This is the time to put out a call for action out of patriotic duty, to close with a moving poem, recount one last inspiring story, or make an assertion that touches on something the audience members are passionate about (children, animals, religion, human rights, Mother Earth, abortion).

E ssential

If you are talking about something complicated, use visual aids and vividly descriptive words to fix your message in the brain's visual memory. Studies show that this is the best way for people to remember what you said.

Let Them Know How to Get More Information

Remind them that there will be handouts at the door (see Chapter 8) and that this will have Web sites and other resources listed, as well as your contact information.

Keep your closing brief or the audience will feel tricked into having paid closer attention. You might even get a standing ovation, if you close with enthusiasm.

CHAPTER 4

Eloquent Sources

An informative or persuasive speech may be effective enough in getting across your message if you follow the basic rules. But if you want to make it more memorable and moving—more eloquent, with features and phrases that stick in the mind and uplift the soul—there are a number of tactics you should master. One is to tell stories that illustrate your points. Another is to quote the colorful and insightful observations of others (preferably the famous) about your topic. Citing poems can also provide an artistic flourish that touches the emotions.

Why Stories

"Why not begin with a story?" asks Dale Carnegie rhetorically in *Public Speaking for Success*. "From ancient times on, storytellers entertained, educated, and enlightened their listeners—from primitive people squatting around a campfire to villagers assembled in the town square. . . . Troubadours sang ballads or recited poems and sagas. . . . We still all want to hear stories."

In her classic handbook for storytellers, *Using Stories and Humor: Grab Your Audience*, Joanna Slan explains that the most memorable speeches appeal to both the logical, or left, side of the brain and the emotional, or right side. "Stories showcase content in an emotional setting," which aids long-term retention, she notes. Anecdotes also give information context, without which it "exists only as clutter" in the mind.

Although you may have been hired to, say, train the members of a workplace team in a technical skill, your audience will unconsciously compare your presentation with television programs, videos, and other forms of entertainment. You can make even the most mundane communication task more interesting by incorporating a story.

When people listen to a tale being related, they match it up in their minds with their own experiences and needs to see if the lessons the speaker draws from these are valid for their own lives. They may not have had anything precisely like that incident happen to them, but there are universal themes a speaker can tap into about the most important issues, such as self-esteem, right priorities, friends and family, overcoming obstacles, the value of a spiritual path, hard work, loyalty, patience, courage, and so forth. If anecdotes are carefully chosen, a majority in the audience will find touchstones of identification that will enable them to internalize your messages. Whether the goals are big or small, a story makes the educational process more entertaining.

E ssential

To develop as a teller of stories in public, learn from those who have been doing it. One way is to join the National Storytelling Network at *www.storynet.org*.

Another reason to incorporate stories into your presentation is that listeners tend to become jaded the longer you talk. A change of pace from giving information to relating a relevant anecdote has a similar effect to altering the loudness of your voice: it will prompt people to wake up and pay closer attention.

And if you have a stock of anecdotes ready, you can add them to your presentation if you need to fill a longer speaking slot than you normally do. You should have alternatives to use as backups. Unless you only use stories that are your own personal experience, a speaker before you may tell the very one you were going to. Also, when you first get a look at the audience, you may realize that it is not well suited to your regular choice—they might be too old or too young to fully appreciate an anecdote about a musician. Or a story about a businesswoman may not be the most appropriate for an audience of retired army officers. Of course, your research should have tipped you to who would be in the audience, but surprises happen.

 Fact

Create different versions of your stories, some longer and some shorter than normal, in case the program gets started late and the moderator informs you that you will only be able to speak twenty minutes instead of thirty. Or maybe you will get a note at the podium to talk an extra five minutes because the next speaker is running late.

Elements of Story Building

An experience that is only superficially recalled is not going to be a tale worth telling because it will not become real to the audience. You want to create a story arc that takes a series of actions that move the plot forward to a dramatic turning point, with a conclusion that is meaningful for your audience. The central character is generally going to need to be sympathetic, so that the audience will easily identify. If that character is you, it is good to be flawed—the worst speakers, in terms of effectiveness, are those who portray themselves as superhuman, someone people will not relate to. The main character needs to confront a challenge and then find a way to resolve it. Start noticing how stories get told in books and movies and on TV (although you will need to boil yours down to no more than a few minutes, of course).

Does the story you tell have to be literally true in every detail? Ask yourself if the people involved in the experience being related would want to be identified by name or if where they live and their profession must be given. Probably not, so you will need to change those facts to protect them anyway (do not ask for permission, since you may get a firm no even to using their disguised descriptions). You may also realize that some aspects of the anecdote could be unnecessarily inflammatory if you mention them—perhaps your villain happens to be an African American or the professor you loved was a member of the Communist Party. Odds are that a lot of the details you could relate would simply distract the audience from absorbing the lessons, so delete those, too. You can see that there is plenty of room for creative design of how you talk about real events.

E *ssential*

Position your stories more or less evenly throughout your speech or they will bunch up and seem to be a string of anecdotes without sufficient explanatory commentary. Too many tales will also begin to bore the audience.

Poetic license is taken in fact-based movies because no one would sit still for the dull details of the actual events. The tale needs to be condensed into two hours to create an interesting story arc. In the few minutes that you have to touch on the highlights of your story, the factual details are almost irrelevant compared with the message you want to convey. On the other hand, do not stray too far from what actually happened or the audience will feel tricked if it finds out. If the main character just spent one night locked up for driving drunk, don't claim he killed someone and went to jail for ten years.

Professional speaker Barry Mann comments, "I am a creative artist and that makes me different from a reporter. Reporters tell facts; storytellers tell truths." Aim for the higher truth in selecting stories and their elements. "Keep to the essential truth of a story, even if the details are stretched," adds Joanna Slan.

A good guide to constructing and delivering stories is Doug Lipman's *The Storytelling Coach*.

Personal Anecdotes

So where can you find stories to tell? The best place would be within your own experience. For one thing, no one else will be relating quite the same tale. And a personal anecdote that the audience can identify with—or maybe just laugh at—will bond them to you. But what if you do not think you have enough interesting personal experiences to relate? Do not be so sure: a little archaeological work is in order. Keep thinking about this over a period of months and you will be surprised at what your subconscious dredges up from forgotten memories.

 Fact

If there is a public-speaking crime, it is lifting someone else's story and pretending it was your experience or creation without crediting the source. It happens all too often, depriving the originator of value, and if the thief is unmasked, word will get around not to hire him.

Write down all your personal traits. Are you mischievous, analytical, romantic, cynical, an eternal optimist, energetic, patriotic, angry, meticulous, emotionally demonstrative, a sports fan, a lover of books, a procrastinator? Take the Myers Briggs personality test at *www.DiscoverYourPersonality.com* or the relationship inventory at *www.eharmony.com* and use these to make up a list of your characteristics. Then periodically concentrate on locating a memory for each—something you did or said that was funny, upsetting, odd, or interesting. Once you have that kernel, spend some time seeing if there is a story, a turning point, and a lesson at the end that could be relevant to your intended audience.

Search your memory by where you spent much of your time. Make a list of every job you ever held and try to recall stories for each one. Think about each year of college. If you were in the military, look at memorabilia that might trigger memories. The same for churches or synagogues, clubs, restaurants, playing fields, and so forth.

E ssential

Watch professional speakers carefully as they relate their anecdotes—where they place them in the presentation, how they develop interest in the characters, the building of tension, the resolution, and how the lesson is made clear. Notice the delivery—pacing, vocal changes, and gestures.

Think about experiences related to events: your birthday or those of family and friends, holidays, vacations, dates, being out with friends, going to the zoo, hiking, and so forth. As Donald Davis says in *Telling Your Own Stories: For Family and Classroom Storytelling, Public Speaking, and Personal Journaling*, getting started is hard, but then, if systematically worked, the memories should come flooding back. What happened when you moved from one home to another? Do you recall being lost as a child?

Talk to others in your life, past and present. Write down what you remember about what happened between the two of you, then call the other person up to see what they recall. Also look at photos, whether in the family photo album or the high school yearbook, to see what memories they stir up.

If you ever kept a diary, glance through it for ideas. You will probably be surprised by reminders of people and events you had moved into the storage area of your mind. If you do not write in a journal now, start doing it and a year or two from now it can become another resource. You do not have to write formal sentences—just a few words to remind you of what was important, especially anything that might become a story you can use later, whether about great customer service or a practical joke that went awry.

Alert

As with all elements of speaking, you want to tape yourself and listen to various ways of telling the same story. Once you have worked out the best wording, videotape yourself or stand in front of a mirror as you give the speech to work on delivery.

Make a list of favorite things past and present—books, movies, music, comedians, TV series, flavors, flowers, cars, and so forth. Each is likely to hold more than one associated story. Your subconscious will begin doing the homework assignment and sending up ideas 24/7. Keep a pen and paper handy wherever you are, including by your bed.

Others' Experiences

You will sound like an egomaniac and bore your audience if you only tell grand tales about yourself as the hero. You can refresh audience interest by making other people the center of your stories. To find them:

- Interview people who are likely to have had interesting experiences related to the topic you are addressing. If you have a hard time finding anyone, post a request for sources at *www .profnet.prnewswire.com*. A message will go out to publicists for colleges, businesses, nonprofit organizations, authors, and others.

- Start looking at the headlines in magazines and newspapers in terms of incidents that will illustrate your messages.
- Read books in the field. Biographies of famous people can be gold mines of amusing and instructive stories. Mention the name of the book and its author, both as a professional courtesy and in case listeners want to learn more.

But before you start using someone else's story, even with appropriate credit, you should do an online search for the author, to see if it is likely that she is out on the speaking circuit and will be using it. If she is cranking out a lot of articles and books, she is probably promoting her most recent examples, so the older anecdotes would be the safest to use. You can also write and ask permission. The author may be delighted to get the plug for the book.

 Fact

When you come to the end of the story, make sure that everyone will understand this most critical phase. Slow down and enunciate. Write it so that some words will not be mistaken for others. You do not want members of the audience turning to those next to them at the crucial moment and asking, "What did she say?"

Using Great Quotations

Quotations can succinctly and colorfully distill an observation about an idea you want to convey in a speech. These get attention first because of the change of pace from your own words.

Second, the person you are quoting is usually going to be some sort of celebrity, which in and of itself gets attention (so mention the name before you start reading the quote). Even if the individual was not really an authority on the subject, her many fans will listen more closely.

Third, the particular phrasing helps the audience remember the point you are making. It may put the idea into an amusing setting.

For these reasons, putting a quotation at the front of your talk is a good way to get off on the right foot with an audience (and if there is a bit of humor involved, all the better to get everyone laughing).

Do not use a long quotation because minds will wander: trim to the essential point if the original wording is long-winded or not entirely relevant to your subject. You can also paraphrase, if you let listeners know you are doing so.

Finding Quotations

What primary references should you use? *Bartlett's Familiar Quotations* is the favorite of many, as is *The Oxford Dictionary of Quotations*. A good source for humorous quotes is *The Penguin Dictionary of Modern Humorous Quotations*.

A more recent entry that draws more on popular culture than traditional volumes is *The Quotionary*, edited by Leonard Roy Frank. You can find pithy comments on, for starters, abortion, AIDS, and American foreign policy. They may come from business consultant Peter Drucker, fantasy novelist Ursula Le Guin, movie director and actor Clint Eastwood, or social philosopher E. F. Schumacher.

You may also find it useful to consult collections that have a particular focus, such as *Success* (edited by J. Pincott), which has quotations about issues like working hard, setting goals, and being fearless.

Among the 193,000 choices of specialized quote collections offered by Amazon are *The Rubicon Dictionary of Positive and*

Motivational Quotations, The Oxford Dictionary of Scientific Quotations, The Music Lover's Quotation Book, The Military Quotation Book, and *African American Quotations.*

Alert

Never rely on the Internet for exact wording or attribution. Quite often even sites devoted to providing accurate quotations and their sources will have misinformation. The Net is useful for coming up with ideas you can double-check with authoritative published quotation volumes.

Use Quotes Appropriately

Here are hints to using quotes appropriately in your speech:

- Use the words of at least one person appropriate to the audience: do not only cite male business leaders to an audience of women entrepreneurs.
- When you speak to international audiences, quote someone from their culture or use proverbs common in that country.
- Make sure you know how to pronounce the name of each person you are quoting.
- Provide some background to the quotation if it will help the audience appreciate the sentiment (such as noting that the comment came just after the author's wife died or he had gone bankrupt).
- Finishing with an inspirational quote is a good way to leave the audience with a positive impression of you and the overall speech.

Also remember that when you read a quotation, do it in a different tone of voice to spark interest and highlight it as separate from the rest of your speech. Say it slowly, since often what makes it memorable is unusual wording. Then pause a few beats, as it will take a few seconds to absorb.

Citing Correct Sources

An astonishing number of often-cited sayings attributed to famous people are incorrectly credited or dubiously attributed, even in the most respected quotation sources. The best research on this subject can be found in Ralph Keyes's *The Quote Verifier*. A few of the lines that are popular with speakers include:

- "America is great because America is good. If America ceases to be good, America will cease to be great." Attributed to Alexis de Tocqueville, but no one really knows who said this.
- "There is a principle which is a bar against all information . . . contempt prior to investigation." Credited to the philosopher Herbert Spencer, it was actually written by theologian William Paley in 1794.
- "You can fool all of the people some of the time; you can fool some of the people all of the time; but you can't fool all of the people all of the time." Always attributed to President Lincoln, there is no evidence that he ever said this and the actual author is unknown.
- "I disapprove of what you say, but will defend to the death your right to say it." This is usually said to be a comment by Voltaire, but this was actually the way Voltaire biographer Evelyn Beatrice Hall portrayed the philosopher's attitude towards the writing of a colleague.
- "If the only tool you have is a hammer, everything looks like a nail." This has been ascribed to everyone from the Buddha to Mark Twain. The original idea was philosopher Abraham Kaplan's, stated in 1964, but this particular wording was formulated two years later by psychologist Abraham Maslow.

Of course, the point of the quotation is not who said it, but the thought, so if you are not sure of the source, just say, "someone once said" or note that it has been put into the mouths of many famous people. Even if you get the source wrong, no one in the audience is likely to care, but you should make some effort to get it right, in case someone does challenge the cited source.

Adding a Poetic Touch

After Shakespeare and the Bible, the greatest source of quotations in *Bartlett's* is the great poets, including Milton, Tennyson, Byron, Keats, Yeats, and Eliot (as well as Emerson, the sole man of prose in this elite group). Of course, much of Shakespeare is poetry, as are parts of the Bible, notably the Songs of Solomon and Psalms.

In many cases, you will just want to use a few lines to put a memorable poetic light on your subject. To that end, you can just look up the name of the poet in the author index of *The Quotionary* and see what topics he commented on (*Bartlett's* has a subject index, but does not show the name of the source there, just part of the line in question, although it is more likely to have more of any given poem). Not all references for the author will be poems; some will be comments on the topic.

For example, in talking about the difference between self-esteem and arrogance, you might quote Milton's "Paradise Lost":

Oft times nothing profits more
Than self-esteem, grounded on just and right
Well manag'd.

A couple of lines from Lord Byron's "Childe Harold's Pilgrimage" have been quoted to put nuclear war in perspective:

A thousand years scarce serve to form a state;
An hour may lay it in dust.

If you have the time, you could quote poems more extensively for a more powerful impact (although you do not want to turn your speech into a poetry reading). It would help in these cases to put up the words for the audience to read along with you, since absorbing the meaning of more than a few poetic lines can be difficult, but avoid anything so cryptic that it needs a lot of explanation.

For example in discussing the need to have faith that times will change, Tennyson wrote, in "In Memoriam A.H.H.":

O, yet we trust somehow good
Will be the final goal of ill . . .
Behold, we know not anything;
I can but trust that good shall fall
At last—far off—at last, to all,
And every winter change to spring.

Yeats acknowledged the benefits of forgiving oneself in "A Dialogue of Self and Soul":

I am content to follow to its source
Every event in action or in thought;
Measure the lot; forgive myself the lot!
When such as I cast out remorse
So great a sweetness flows into the breast
We must laugh and we must sing,
We are blest by everything,
Everything we look upon is blest.

CHAPTER 5

Refining Touches

Y ou have done the first draft of a speech that makes its key points within an appropriate framework. You may have included a couple of anecdotes and famous quotations or even a poem. Now it is time to go over it once more for polishing, making sure it is clear, and adding some sophisticated techniques like alliteration, allusion, and metaphors.

The Need for Revision

It is human nature to want to get a difficult job done as quickly as possible. But every successful writer knows that one of the differences between a professional and an amateur is the amount of revision. Even after a pro has gone over the first draft of an article carefully and believes it is ready to submit to the editor, she will sleep on it another day or two, if there is time. Inevitably, in the light of another day, there is a new perspective and fresh information to make it even better. Sometimes, a writer will go through this process several times until she cannot think of another significant improvement. The same approach applies to the ideal way to write a speech. The longer you have to finish it, the more opportunity you have to do more research and refine it (not to mention to practice more).

For a persuasive speech, you want to step back and reexamine whether you present the arguments in a logical order. Following a structure—like simple-to-complex or chronological—does not guarantee that each point starts solidly on the prior argument. Often, speakers make overly optimistic assumptions about what the audience will buy into before considering the next idea. Show the first draft to someone who disagrees with its point of view, to see whether they can poke holes in its logic.

Alert

Do not get hung up on rigidly following "proper grammar," just speak in a normal conversational way. Ignore the rule, for example, that forbids ending a sentence with a preposition and would have you say "this is the subject about which we are going to talk," instead of "this is the subject we are going to talk about."

If you have a personal attorney or a friend who is a lawyer, she would be useful to use as a sounding board. Law students are taught critical thinking, which allows them to analyze a proposition and then construct arguments pro and con.

Also, look at how you refer to people in the speech from the standpoint of gender usage. Do not try to be neutral by always using the sexless "one could do that." Unless you are speaking of an actual individual, alternate "he" and "she" so that you do not consistently leave one part of the audience out of your references and you retain the sense of a real person. When it comes to terms that have been traditionally sexist, use what will seem most natural for today: businesswoman instead of businessperson or police officer instead of policewoman. In some cases, either the old or the new will be acceptable: chairwoman or chairperson or even just chair.

Simplification and Clarity

By definition, you are invited to give a speech because the group believes you have knowledge to share, which many in the audience will not already have. It is vital that you get some kind of assessment about the level of awareness the majority have about your topic or you may talk over their heads. If most are not experts on the fundamentals of your subject, be sure you avoid jargon and references to technical issues that are not explained.

E ssential

Overworked cliches should be avoided, like "cool as a cucumber" or "live and learn." However, you can use one to good effect in a funny context, like a box-maker which "thinks outside the box" to come up with a different product line, or the "light at the end of the tunnel is an oncoming freight train of change." Or you can reverse the traditional advice: "the customer is *not* always right."

Give the big picture of what you will be talking about in your opening, then make sure the transitions between your subtopics are logical and smooth. You can summarize what you have just said at the end of each section and then link it to the next point. "Now that we understand what the expectations for NAFTA were, let's examine how it measured up since implementation." This is also a way to regularly tell the audience to pay attention, to counter its never-ending downward cycle into boredom.

For all but the most technical presentations, use words most people will know, rather than brainier ones—results, instead of output; clarify, instead of elucidate; speed, instead of expedite. If you show off by using obscure words, those who do not know them will be puzzled and to the rest you will sound pretentious.

Do not use foreign-language words or phrases without translation, even those you feel everyone should know (*caveat emptor*, *esprit de corps*). In all likelihood, some portion of the audience will be confused.

Some other tips include:

- Eliminate phrases your tongue will trip over.
- Use shorter sentences. Most of Lincoln's Gettysburg Address consists of sentences of five words or less.
- Simplify phrases. For example, instead of "in a majority of cases" you could just say "usually," or you could substitute "during" for "in the course of."
- Be as precise as possible because the audience will impose very different ideas—"sometime" might mean next week or next year, "near" could be interpreted as twenty miles or five miles away.
- Be bold, rather than using vague words. Instead of "we will take this under consideration next week," say "we will make a decision next week."
- Avoid euphemisms, like "collateral damage" instead of "civilian casualties" or "ill-advised move" instead of a "poor" one.
- Make sure that any acronyms are understood by everyone— SEC for Securities and Exchange Commission, DWP for Department of Water and Power, etc.
- Get to the point. Nothing bores an audience more than a windbag who talks and talks without moving the meaty content forward.

Vivid Language

One key difference between professional and amateur writers—and speakers—is how they handle the use of descriptive words. Most amateurs do not use words that are descriptive enough—they might say that a woman wore a provocative outfit, without indicating it was a short dress of a certain color or even a dress at all. On the other hand, those who begin to understand the need to describe more precisely often go overboard and relate every possible detail of someone's attire to the point that it distracts from the flow of the narrative.

Another important way to give a speech sparkle is to use the active voice, in which the subject takes an action. Instead of the passive "the boy was bitten by the dog," you would say "the dog bit the boy." Active is usually more concise and often clearer in meaning and easier to remember.

Use imagery that appeals to any of the senses, which helps make the idea more real and lodges it more effectively in the memory. You might refer to "the laughter as the family passed around the Thanksgiving dishes of turkey, stuffing, and sweet potato." Be as concrete as possible, which will enable listeners to instantly see what you mean, instead of having to translate the word into an image. Describe someone going to Kmart, instead of a department store.

E ssential

Highly successful Republican pollster Frank Luntz, in *Words That Work: It's Not What You Say, It's What People Hear*, provides a formula for power persuasion: small words, short sentences, be consistent and credible, speak to people's aspirations, provide context and explain relevance, and use visual imagery.

Use dramatic words, like wild, unusual, powerful, enormous, horrendous, evil, devastated, immediately, and extraordinary. These prod the audience to pay more attention to what you are describing. Use the strongest action verb possible—"he ran to the mailbox," instead of "he went"; "she screamed," instead of "raised her voice."

Allusion

In literature, allusion is a subtle reference to an object or event, which depends on the sophisticated reader to recognize it. The densest example is James Joyce's *Finnegan's Wake*, about which entire volumes have been written to explain its historic and literary references. Poets like Virgil used allusion to pack a lot of power into a few words. More familiar today would be this technique as used in films. Directors may slyly allude to movies they admire by creating dialogue or scenes that imitate them in a way that fans will recognize (known as *homage*). In these cases, allusion provides a sense of depth and context, and the new work becomes associated with the emotion and ideas of the original.

Fact

According to Jim Canterucci, author of *Personal Brilliance: Managing the Everyday Habits that Create a Lifetime of Success*, only 35 percent of Americans have read a book since high school. And 20 percent say they have never been in a bookstore. This creates a barrier to the use of allusions to literature.

For speakers, the purpose would need to be simpler and more obvious to a wider group, providing resonance with a well-known aspect of culture. The Reverend Martin Luther King Jr. began his "I Have a Dream" speech with, "Five score years ago," an obvious allusion to President Lincoln's Gettysburg Address opening, "Four score and seven years ago . . ." The purpose was to suggest a parallel crossroads for the nation in these two struggles, the Civil War and the movement for civil rights for African Americans.

With Americans reading fewer books, magazines, and newspapers and knowing less and less about history and literature, allusion has challenging limits today. But most everyone will know the basic idea behind references to Pandora's box or "between a rock and a hard place," even though these allude to Greek mythology. Certain expressions from pop culture are so widely known (such as the Wicked Witch of the West or Catch-22) that they can be safely used, often tongue-in-cheek. If you have time to let your speech gestate, your subconscious may bring up such cross-references and listeners who understand them will appreciate your presentation on another level.

Antonyms, Rhyme, Alliteration

Professional speechwriters like to deploy words and phrases that play off one another to make them delightful to the ear and memorable.

Antonyms

Antonyms are words that are opposites of each other and provide contrast, like day and night, slow and fast, teacher and student, hot and cold.

Winston Churchill was fond of antonyms, as cited in James Humes's *Speak Like Churchill, Stand Like Lincoln*:

- "There is only one answer to defeat and that is victory."
- "This is not the end, nay, not even the beginning of the end, but it is, perhaps, the end of the beginning."
- "If the present quarrels with the past, surely the future will already have been lost."

Benjamin Franklin also used them in many of his sayings ("never leave that for tomorrow which you can do today").

Rhyme

Among the examples of internal rhyme that Churchill used:

- "Out of intense complexities, intense simplicities emerge. Humanity, not legality, should be our guide."
- "Those professional intellectuals who revel in decimals and polysyllables . . ."

Likewise, Franklin incorporated rhymes in many of his maxims:

- "Early to bed, early to rise, makes a man healthy, wealthy, and wise."
- "An apple a day keeps the doctor away."

Muhammad Ali built his career around using rhyme to create memorable sound bites. Ali once explained his ring strategy as, "I outwit them and then I out-hit them." Some have speculated that his style helped launch rap music, since its power rests largely on the rhymes of the spoken word.

Humes says that speechwriters often turn to nine word-endings "for coining 'zinger' lines": ame (blame, claim), air (bear, care), ite (bite, cite), ake (ache, break), ow (dough, flow), ay (day, pray), ate (date, fate), eem (beam, cream), ain (gain, pain).

Alliteration

In alliteration, the same consonant sound repeats consecutively, as in "Peter Piper picked a peck of pickled peppers." Less heavy-handed use is common in advertising: Holiday Inn's "pleasing people the world over" and Land Rover's "the best four-by-four by far." It can convey a sense of lightheartedness. You can use it for the title of a talk: "God Grants Goodness" or "Alleviating Arthritis Alternatively." Again, the goal is to make a phrase memorable and entertaining.

Analogies, Metaphors, Similes

The comparison of one familiar thing with another in order to promote understanding has been a rhetorical device for thousands of years. The following are some of the most common comparisons.

Analogies

Analogies make comparisons between two sets of items: "shoe is to foot as tire is to wheel." The purpose is to clarify the relationships; they do not have to be precisely the same, point by point. An analogy could be made between two things, one of which is familiar, shedding light on the other: "a heart is like a pump" assumes that everyone knows how a pump works. The pairings can be antonyms, synonyms, descriptive (blue is to sky as red is to fire truck), part to whole (arm-body), or item to category (milk-beverage).

Metaphors

A metaphor implies that two very different things have the same properties and is more assertive than an analogy. It substitutes one for the other, making them essentially identical: "you are my sunshine." A well-known extended metaphor is from Shakespeare's *As You Like It*:

All the world's a stage,
And all the men and women merely players;
They have their exits and their entrances;
And as one man plays many parts,
His acts being seven ages. At first the infant,
Mewling and puking in the nurse's arms.
And then the whining school-boy, with his satchel,
And shining morning face, creeping like snail
Unwillingly to school. And then the love . . .

There are many types of metaphors. The answer to the famous riddle of the Sphinx is an example of a conceptual one, a metaphor that is systematic: What goes on four legs in the morning, two legs at midday, and three in the evening? A man—crawling as a baby, then upright, then using a cane in old age.

Similes

Similes are similar to metaphors, except that in a simile the comparison is made explicit by using the words "like" or "as." Instead of "you are my sunshine," a simile would state this as "you are like sunshine to me."

Other common similes:

- Sly as a fox
- Like playing with fire
- Clean as a whistle
- Hard as nails
- Pretty as a picture

Hyperbole takes the comparison and exaggerates it. "I had to wait for what felt like forever" would be a simile, while hyperbole would phrase it as "I had to wait forever."

Repetition

As in advertising, repeating a message is one of the keys to keeping it on the brain's radar screen. You can use different words, other examples, or fresh analogies. As the great Irish orator Daniel O'Connell stated regarding his campaign for Catholic emancipation in the early nineteenth century: "It is not by advancing a political truth once or twice, or even ten times, that the public will take it up and adopt it. Incessant repetition is required to impress political truths upon the mind."

You can also repeat words and phrases as a rhetorical device that links the components of the speech together to create a theme, as Martin Luther King did in his most famous speech, "I Have a Dream," delivered on the steps of the Lincoln Memorial in Washington, D.C., in 1963. Most people are familiar with his nine-time repetition of "I have a dream" from the middle of the speech, but he also used repetition elsewhere in the speech, for example the reiteration of the words, "Let freedom ring" in the last lines.

Dr. King's speech is one of the most memorable in American political history, not only because he was eloquent about such an important subject, but because he knew the human mind will best retain concepts that are repeated in various ways.

CHAPTER 6

You're Only Joking

Humor can improve a speech better than anything else because it gets the audience to react positively to you. A joke will also help the audience remember a serious point you want to make. But this is the trickiest part of a speech, since everyone's taste is different and few speakers have mastered comic delivery. There are easy ways to lighten up a talk by borrowing the right jokes. You can also improve your own sense of humor with more effort and create some lines no one has heard before.

Start with a Bit of Wit

"A little levity will save many a speech from sinking," observed Samuel Butler, the nineteenth-century British novelist. Applying it right at the beginning will break the ice. The audience may be uneasy about the subject you are going to address, and you can dispel the tension with laughter. They may be skeptical about your credentials, and you can make them more receptive by being likable. Or they could just be bored after a series of speeches and need to be perked up.

The opening jest does not need to be professional grade. If the audience does not know you, expectations will be low, so the first joke may get a better reaction than later attempts at humor. But you want to put the most thought into this one because any misfire will make it more likely they will tune out from that point on (which is why some speakers warn against putting humor up-front).

An amusing anecdote is a proven crowd pleaser at the beginning of a speech. Keep it short, so that you get to the punch line before attention wanders. If you can localize elements of a standard tale, you are likely to get a stronger response—a cop becomes the city's police chief, a generic congressman becomes their representative.

E ssential

Funny definitions can get laughter from almost any group. Ambrose Bierce, in *The Devil's Dictionary*, defined an egotist as "a person of low taste, more interested in himself than me." Contempt, he said, is the feeling of "a prudent man for an enemy who is too formidable safely to be opposed."

Self-deprecation also works well as an opener because it shows you have the confidence to have the audience laugh at and with you. Abraham Lincoln was berated by a debate opponent as being a two-faced politician. Lincoln's opening response was, "Friends, I ask you, if I were two-faced, would I be wearing this one?"

Study the opening lines of other speakers (not comics) and make notes about what types of humor received the best response. You can convert their approach into openers for your speeches.

Know the Audience's Sense of Humor

You are appearing on a local TV talk show about gardening to discuss your experiences. You have been asked to speak to a Veterans of Foreign Wars chapter in favor of a candidate for Congress.

Each of these venues would provide an opportunity for some levity to bond with the audience. But if you do not give sufficient attention to your choice of humor, you could get into trouble right away. On the talk show, you make a crack about another expert who "obviously hasn't been outdoors in a few years" (not realizing she is a favorite of viewers). At the VFW, you remark that the opposing candidate should take advantage of his proposed healthcare program to get a spine transplant (although he is a veteran and your candidate is not).

 **Alert**

William Shakespeare said, "A jest's prosperity lies in the ear of he who hears it, not in the tongue of him that makes it." You might think a line is funny, but your audience does not and could even be offended. Test with someone who knows local taste before you jest from the podium.

A little research would help avoid getting off on the wrong foot (and then putting it in your mouth). In the case of TV, you should watch the show, listen to callers, and ask the host about her audience and recent guests and topics. In cases like the VFW speech, you can study the organization's Web site and your opponent's position papers before speaking, not just your own candidate's information. If you can get to an event early or there is a dinner, chat with the guests. If you are speaking out of town, look at the local newspaper's Web site.

Watch Your Tongue

Unless you know the audience very well and have spoken to it before, there are danger zones to avoid. Obviously, race, ethnicity, handicaps, religion, and sex are minefields. Additionally, a whole range of other areas can be politically incorrect for different audiences, from jokes about women to weight.

That does not mean you can never joke about stereotypes. Someone of Irish heritage who is involved with the local Irish community year round (not just on March 17) can get away with citing the late

Pat O'Brien's comment that "it's a good thing that God created whiskey. It kept the Irish from ruling the world."

 **Alert**

Political audiences love to laugh at their opponents' alleged beliefs and can get an equal kick being teased about their own stereotypes. But post-9/11, you have to be careful about the types of jokes you make about terrorism and patriotism.

Some occasions, like a funeral, are solemn, but that does not mean humor has no place. Friends may recall funny things the deceased said or did and make laughter part of the grieving process. But it would not be advisable for a stranger to crack a joke that was not very well informed by friends or family.

As a rule, never use profanity from the podium. Think of yourself as on radio, where performers restrict themselves to avoid FCC fines and can still be entertaining.

Good-Natured Insults

Don Rickles and Joan Rivers draw sell-out crowds for their outrageous insults. It is unlikely you could pull that off, so do not make the attempt just to be different from other speakers. But if you feel you know the boundaries for the group you will be addressing, you might get away with some ribbing. Maybe the company manager is a clothes horse and always late for meetings, so you can comment that she has a good excuse: she has to make a costume change between scenes. Or the Board of Directors has decided to make sure she is presentable as a spokesperson for the company, so it is now allocating 25 percent of its profit for her wardrobe. Or she is late because she is frugal: she did not want to spend money on this year's calendar.

Give Me a Break!

Hopefully, you are off to a good start and know what type of humor will work for your audience. How often do you need to throw in something fun? You certainly do not want to give the impression that you just tacked on someone else's joke at the beginning because that is what you were expected to do. Odds are, though, listeners are not expecting a laugh-a-thon; you just need to occasionally lighten up a straightforward talk. Even Shakespearian tragedies have comic relief to make the heaviness tolerable. Too much seriousness can also put people to sleep, so you need to find points to insert something upbeat.

After you decide how to open, just work on your speech without reference to giving it humor breaks. If something occurs to you that seems to fit in, make a note, but just get a rough first draft done so you can see how long it will take to deliver the material you absolutely need to cover within the time limit. Then look at it for potential openings for a little levity, perhaps every five or ten minutes. These do not have to be full-blown jokes—a wry comment or a sarcastic observation will engage the audience.

"Brevity is the soul of wit," said Shakespeare. Your jokes should be short enough to memorize because reading drains the life out of them. Ultimately, what matters is whether the audience feels that the time taken to tell your joke was worthwhile. When in doubt, cut the unnecessary detail to get to the punch line quicker.

Underscoring an important point you want people to remember with humor is the ideal way to deploy it. It can take an abstract idea and make it concrete. If you say something amusing and it has a graphic element, describing it vividly will help it stick in the minds of your listeners.

Do not use humor that is not in some way relatable to the overall message you are delivering. Everyone has heard too many jokes told to open a speech, which then goes in an entirely different direction. Tacking on that kind of humor artificially will not help you succeed and it may hurt if it flops.

Yes, a Borrower Be

George Bernard Shaw asserted, "Good writers borrow. Great writers steal." No humor is entirely original; it builds on forms and sources going back thousands of years. Most one-liners and funny stories have come up from the grassroots and are not attributable. A comic draws on a subconscious filled with these things to put together new material. However, you do not want to be thought of as pretending that you made up something entirely on your own when a lot of people know otherwise, so either adapt the details of a joke to fit your point or acknowledge the source (even "someone has said").

If you only need to lighten your talks occasionally, do not put a lot of effort into it. But if you expect to be giving a lot of speeches and need to change the comic bits because some in the audience may have already heard you, at least the process will be fun. Start your own topical humor file by clipping out the good items and filing them on index cards (you will rarely want anything longer than two sides). There are almost endless sources.

The Net

At *www.100topjoke.com* there is an aggregate of useful sites, including those covering such humor-challenged topics as philosophy, science, and economics ("an economist is a trained professional paid to guess wrong about the economy"). If you want any-occasion laughs about lawyers, blondes, men, animals, and other subjects, *www.cleanjoke.com* is great. Also *www.jokesgalore.com* offers a daily joke e-mail service and claims to be the world's largest repository of jokes, including ones on touchy topics.

To find the right gag that is both funny and apropos, expect to put in some research time. Fortunately, you do not need a lot to make your speech just amusing enough to keep most audiences engaged.

 Fact

You can google "jokes" and come up with 60 million hits and "humor" yields 250 million. Most of these are not very useful for speakers—they include everything from official sites of comic strips to homemade prank videos—but no matter what your talk is about, you will probably find a site devoted to it.

Magazines and Newspapers

Reader's Digest is the king and queen of magazine humor, with its reader-supplied items for a variety of categories every month (and reading it is a great way to keep tabs on popular culture, which is an essential practice for every speaker).

The art of speech humor often involves describing a visual situation, so the funny pages of newspapers are also a good source. If you are looking for over-the-top spoofs of trends, look at *Mad Magazine*, or for political satire check out *The Onion*.

Books

There are new compilations of humor published every year, but here are some tried-and-tested sources for spicing up your speech:

- *1001 Funniest Things Ever Said* edited by Steven Price. Example: "Give me a couple of years, and I'll make that actress an overnight success"—Samuel Goldwyn. (You could use this to underscore how outsiders never realize all the preparatory work that goes into achieving goals.)

- *Comedy Comes Clean: A Hilarious Collection of Wholesome Jokes, Quotes and One-Liners* edited by Adam Christing. Jay Leno, Bill Cosby, Bob Newhart, and fifty others provide wit that can be deployed in front of any audience. Example: "I have no respect for gangs today. They just drive by and shoot people. At least in the old days, like in *West Side Story*, the gang used to dance with each other first"—Robert G. Lee. (Use this to talk about how people romanticize the past.)

- *Winning with One-Liners: 3,400 Hilarious Laugh Lines* edited by Pat Williams. Lots of clean humor, especially about sports, diets, and business. Example: "Dolphins are so smart that in only a few weeks of captivity, they can train people to stand at the edge of a pool and throw them fish"—anonymous. (This could illustrate differing perspectives on the relationship between suppliers and customers.)

- *The Friars Club Encyclopedia of Jokes* edited by H. Alan Cohl. Much of this would not be usable for sensitive audiences, since the Club's roasts were often bawdy. But everyone in your audience will know the contributors, from Mae West to Groucho Marx. Example: "For the first year of marriage, I had a basically bad attitude. I tended to place my wife underneath a pedestal"—Woody Allen. (This could be used to talk about how attitudes can shape results.)

Hire a Writer

The above sources can give you more options to get your audience chuckling than you could ever possibly use. But perhaps you need help because you are addressing an obscure topic with little relationship to the generic humor that is available (hay does not seem to be the subject of many jokes, so you may need help if you are speaking at an animal feed convention). Or maybe you plan to give a lot of speeches and want to have some original material without making a personal effort. Or you could be expected to deliver a real yuk-fest at a high-profile roast and would feel more confident with help. Veteran joke writer Gene Perret, in *How to Hold Your Audience with Humor*, suggests these guidelines for working with a professional:

- Ask a prospect for a couple of pages of material they already have written that might have even a distant relation to what you need.
- If you want to audition them to address your subject specifi- cally, pay for their time. No real pro is going to waste any effort on auditioning, since getting the gig is always a long shot.
- Provide as much preparatory material to the writer as you can—your speech as far as you have written it, some of your prior speeches (even on other topics), talks by others to the same audience, background on the industry, and so on. Studying all this has to be factored into the time the writer will spend on the project.
- If you need five good jokes, contract for twenty. Discuss what you like and dislike about each and the writer can rewrite them. Even then, many will not work for you, for a variety of reasons (they rely on puns that will go over the heads of too many in the audience, too many cross the line of good taste, the writer does not really understand the business, etc.).
- You can pay per joke, per speech, or put the writer on retainer (which would be a very modest investment for a professional speaker to have a reliable source).
- Do a lot of stroking. Anyone working in a creative field will have some level of insecurity, so thank them profusely for their efforts and make criticism constructive.

You can find a professional gag writer in a number of ways. Post a project offer at sites for freelance writers like *www.asja.org*. Google "joke writing service" and you will get 2.5 million options. Run a classified ad in a trade magazine for the industry you regularly address or in *Hollywood Reporter* or *Variety*—many comedy writers can adapt their humor style to almost any subject. Best of all, perhaps, is to advertise in Perret's "Round Table Comedy Newsletter" at *www.comedywriting.com.*

Develop Your Sense of Humor

You already know you have plenty of material to choose from in written sources and with the option of hiring a writer. But neither of these approaches precludes developing your own funny bone so that you can more easily come up with your own ideas to lighten your presentations. Simply making yourself more aware of the kinds of humor out there will allow you to notice what you passively laughed at before and help you develop your own gags. And your subconscious will be equipped to ad-lib if an unexpected situation arises (if the microphone goes out, you can say that "obviously someone is trying to give me a hint to shut up already" or "that's the last time I'll work for a group that didn't pay for more than twenty minutes' use of the mike").

Watch Comedy
Television and movie scripts are not things you can readily borrow from to insert quips into your speech about industrial management. But watching sit-coms and comedies more attentively can help you notice what people laugh at and may inspire your own lines. Alas, reality TV, game shows, and police dramas have moved network sit-coms to the side in recent years, but there are always old episodes of recent hits on the cable channel TBS, or you can rent many classics on DVD.

Movies do not have the same need for rapid, funny dialogue to hold the audience between commercials, but comedy is ascendant, with hot stars like Will Ferrell, Ben Stiller, Adam Sandler, Eddie Murphy, Owen Wilson, Robin Williams, and Jim Carrey. Or watch classics like *Annie Hall, The Odd Couple,* and *Some Like It Hot.*

Pick your favorite late-night TV host—Letterman, Leno, Ferguson, O'Brien, Kimmel—and listen to how they set up and deliver their lines, written with top comedy writers.

On National Public Radio, listen to "Car Talk," "Wait, Wait, Don't Tell Me," or "Whadya Know?"

 ## Question

What do great comedians have in common?
They each have a distinct style they have mined. That is also true of all the late, great humorists from Will Rogers to Rodney Dangerfield. Make your style your own, something you are comfortable with that expresses your distinctive personality.

Read Funny

If you are not already in the habit of reading the comics over breakfast, start your day looking on the bright side and find one strip whose humor can inspire you. Notice visual humor you can describe and translate into something related to your speech subject.

Pick up books by writers like Dave Barry, Andy Borowtiz, Nora Ephron, Douglas Adams, Art Buchwald, David Sedaris, and Erma Bombeck to borrow or adapt their stories and observations. Or if you want to dig deep into the great wits of history, check out Aristophanes, Oscar Wilde, and Mark Twain.

Constructing Jokes

Even if you are not much of a joke-teller in social situations, you can learn to write fresh gags for your speeches. Pick any topic and punch it into the Internet and you will get more starting points than you can imagine ("peanut jokes" gets nearly a million hits).

Gene Perret suggests that you take jokes from books and simply adapt them to your purposes. He also recommends these approaches:

- Write down everything you can think of that is interesting about a topic—nothing has to be funny in and of itself, but look for the odd angles.
- Pair items that are similar or dissimilar.
- Exaggerate and take things to their logical extreme ("if Noah took every type of insect on board, then imagine what it must have been like . . .").
- State a truth in an unusual way—something on people's minds. As George Bernard Shaw said, "If I want to tell a joke, I tell the truth: there's nothing funnier."
- Attack authority or criticize someone who is supposed to be untouchable. Irreverence will likely provoke a laugh.
- Tell a story that is supposed to be a personal experience, then stretch the truth. You localize it by knowing audience pet peeves and things they are proud of, which will make it even funnier to them. Have a few one-liners leading up to the main punch line.

If you really want to get serious about giving fun speeches, you could even benefit from studying the art of writing humor. *How to Write Funny* edited by John Kachuba is the best guide, twenty-nine chapters from masters of comedy like Tom Bodett, Andrei Codrescu, Jennifer Crusie, and Lois-Ann Yamanaka. Among the ideas the masters suggest are to think of an incongruous situation and treat it straight, or to provide a formula with limitless variations (the books in Teddy Kennedy's library, top-ten lists, a twenty-five-second version of *War and Peace*).

In *Comedy Writing Secrets*, Melvin Helitzer lists some formulas that can be used, including plays on words (takeoffs and cliché reformulations), malaprops (misused words), reverses (a switch of viewpoints at the end of the joke), and pairing of two logical, but unconventional ideas. Types of humor discussed include irony (using words to mean the opposite of their normal meaning or a juxtaposition of contrasting elements), satire ("humor with a moral"), and parody (imitating a literary style, but it could also be as simple as making up a phony bestseller list).

E ssential

John Vorhaus, author of *The Comic Toolbox*, flips the usual advice about telling the humorous truth. He advises to tell a lie about an unfunny truth, through exaggeration: "This line is so long, it's going to be getting its own zip code."

Special Delivery

Obviously, you need to rehearse the joke until it goes smoothly. Listen to tapes of your delivery. If you trip over the words, rewrite them to make them easier to say.

Even if you are reading the rest of your speech, this has to be memorized to work or it will seem as if you do not have enough sense of humor of your own so that you need to insert someone else's. An anecdote does not have to be memorized if you can simply hit the main points and remember the punch line.

Speak clearly, strongly, and deliver the punch line with energy while you smile (unless deadpan is appropriate). And remember that when you are done, do not return to giving your speech until the audience's laughter has died down.

And if you have done your homework and rehearsed adequately, a well-developed sense of humor will never leave you without a good ad lib in an awkward moment.

CHAPTER 7

Managing the Audience

Some audiences are easier than others. People may be falling asleep after a meal or too raucous after cocktails. Others might appear bored to death or do not laugh at your jokes. There might even be a heckler, someone who challenges statements and will not wait for the end of the lecture to get answers. On the other hand, everything could go smoothly during the presentation, but you undercut a positive impression by a poorly handled question-and-answer session. Preparation can help you manage these situations.

Get the Audience to Pay Attention

If you are speaking right after lunch or dinner, members of the audience may be a little sleepy because a big meal requires a lot of the body's energy to digest. Late in any all-day seminar, you are probably going to experience audience fatigue: their brains are overflowing with information and it is hard to make room for more. You cannot really change your presentation, except to make it a little crisper by deleting a few details and adding some extra energy. To revive the group before you start, try this approach:

- Acknowledge the challenge of staying interested at that time of day.
- Have everyone stand up and do deep breathing exercises.
- Have a few witty lines ready to get them laughing ("I apologize for waking any of you up before your nap was over . . .").

- Once they sit down, tell them you want everyone to write down, right then, the three most important things to take away (even if you have a handout to give out at the end).

 Fact

Don't take it personally if people doze off. They may have been pulling an all-nighter at the office, may be suffering from jet lag, or had a restless night worrying about a family problem. If you wrote a brilliant speech and practiced your delivery 100 times, a segment in your audience is not going to be paying attention anyway, even with their eyes open.

Later in the presentation, engage the audience in interactivity, such as asking them to raise their hands as you do a survey. How many of them believe customer service at their companies could be improved? How many plan to travel outside the United States in the next two years? But be careful not to ask them to show their feelings about a sensitive issue that could get them in trouble afterward ("how many of you think your firm has incompetent management?").

Or ask for volunteers to come up on stage to interview them about some aspect of the subject—there will always be those who love the limelight, and this will help reengage the audience.

Finally, increase your vocal dynamics to decrease the hypnotic effect of your normal tone—mimic voices of characters in your story, make sound effects, shout, use a "stage whisper," move your voice up and down the range.

The Grumpy Audience

The crowd may only be there because they are required to attend, so acknowledge that. Tell them how what you are about to say will make a big difference in their lives if they implement your recommendations.

If you know they are waiting to hear the speaker after you, mention that you are excited to hear him, too, and are going to offer some ideas that will support what he is about to say.

They may already have heard someone else address your topic. If you did your speech-preparation research, you will have a good idea what the other speakers will have talked about and will have aimed your remarks in a different direction (try to attend similar presentations to be sure). Tell the audience you have some fresh views to share, even disagreements with what they heard previously.

If the audience is known to be opposed to your views, try to find common ground to build rapport. You may disagree about abortion, for example, but can agree on the need to prevent unwanted pregnancies. Be sure you treat the specifics of their views respectfully, even as you explain why you disagree. Never be combative, arrogant, or triumphalist ("now that we have the political upper hand, we'll be repealing those initiatives you rammed through the legislature").

Structuring Q&A

Unless you are giving a keynote address at a dinner or are one of a rotation of brief speakers at a convention, the odds are you will be asked to answer audience questions. At a seminar, where you may be talking for twenty to ninety minutes, you will have the chance either right after you speak or at the end of the session. On the other hand, if you are talking to a small group at a business meeting, it may be expected that you take questions before moving on to each next topic. If you are teaching an all-day seminar, you will need to let the audience speak up after each segment. Whatever the format is, it needs to be agreed on in advance with your host, who should help you manage the audience.

There are three keys to making it likely that everyone will stick to the structure. First, have the host let everyone know what it is before you start, giving it the official stamp of approval. Second, she should tell the audience to write down their questions as they come to mind so they do not forget and are not distracted by trying to remember and listen at the same time. This can help ensure there will actually be questions at the end. Third, if there are people who interrupt at an inappropriate time, the host should remind listeners of the plan. If you are on your own, you have to take care of this yourself. Smile when you lay down the rules and enforce them. Explain that one reason you want questions saved until the end is that your presentation will answer most of them. Of course, interruptions can also break the rhythm of your speech and cause you to forget your next point.

 Question

Should you take written questions?
Written questions may be necessary if the audience is too large or a moderator wants to select the best questions to divide up among panelists, for example. This method does, however, stifle impromptu questions and is a less lively process.

Ideally, the host or panel moderator will pick those who get to ask questions, so you do not get blamed for anyone who is not called on. In some situations, audience members will just come up to a microphone in the aisle. If you have control over who gets to ask, choose individuals from each area of the room. You do not have to do this in a rigid rotation; if someone seems especially eager to talk, waving his hand, it is okay to let him speak up before moving to the next section of the room. If someone has a second question, ask her to wait until others have had their first chance.

Always repeat the question, in case others in the room could not hear it and for the benefit of those who may buy the recording. If the question was put in a rambling or unclear way, restate it to be sure you understand what they are asking. If the question was hostile, rephrase it so that it will fit better with the answer you are about to give. "Why do you have the worst environmental record in the nation?" becomes "You want to know what we are doing to show our concern for the environment," and then acknowledge mistakes and focus on new initiatives.

E ssential

If someone asks about something that was covered in the speech, there is no need to ask why she was not paying attention. You can just say, "To refresh everyone's memory about this issue, let me summarize the essence of what we discussed earlier" or click on a slide that provides the information for anyone who did not see it the first time.

Watch the time to end the session, since some may want to leave to attend another panel and may be embarrassed to get up before your segment is over. Or they may need to go home. In any event, the audience for the next program will want to come into the room. Close to the end of your session, try to end on a positive note with a solid answer and then invite everyone else to talk with you afterward or to give you his card for an e-mail exchange. Do not wait until you pick the very last hand that is up to announce that this will be the last question—it might be an embarrassing one.

Keep the responses brief so that as many people as possible can ask questions. Many Q&A sessions have to end before even a small number have had a chance to participate.

Anticipating Questions

If you have given this presentation several times, you have probably heard most of the related questions. This allows you to work out the perfect answers, with memorable phrases and without repeating what you already said in the speech. You might want to illustrate a point you barely touched on with an anecdote or example. Rehearse these answers as well as the formal presentation. Other hints include:

- Ask colleagues and authorities in the field what questions they commonly get on the same subject.
- Scan new books for points you have not addressed in your speech.
- Read trade journals more closely.
- Think about what else you might have covered if your allotted time had been twice as much.
- Bring documentation you can refer to in order to support your arguments, like the detailed results of a survey you may have just alluded to.

E ssential

Leave a couple of obvious questions unanswered to be sure you get some response, which will stimulate others to think of questions. If there are no questions, you can always say, "One of the most common things people ask me about . . . ," which will give them more time to think about what they might want to ask.

If the question asked is really irrelevant, politely say that that subject is beyond the bounds of what people came to the lecture to talk about and point to the next person with her hand up.

Handling Hostile Questions

Assume the worst: that a critic will ask you the one question you would rather not answer in public. "Isn't it true that you were convicted of stealing ten years ago?" or "Why does your company have the highest number of sexual harassment lawsuits in the state?" If there is a formal, written response available, summarize the main points and offer to e-mail the full document. If you cannot talk about it for legal reasons, say so, but provide a reassuring statement about concern for the important matters at issue.

Never duck a tough question. Give the best answer you can think of and bridge to a related topic that is your strong suit.

Never give an answer that is not honest. Someone in the audience may call you out and your credibility and the effectiveness of your speech will be destroyed on the spot. If you really do not know the answer, tell the questioner that you will need to do research and get back to him. Audiences will tolerate humility in ignorance, but not arrogance. Or you can ask if anyone in the audience knows the answer: this can make that person look smart without this being at your expense, since no one else probably knew the answer, either.

On the other hand, if someone clearly has an in-depth knowledge of the field and disagrees with you, you can simply state that the experts you rely on have a different consensus and note that there are usually disagreements among experts in any field.

Sometimes you may be asked a question based on a false premise: "Have you stopped beating your spouse?" Stay calm and state that you are going to clear up some obvious confusion about the facts in this case.

Another problem can be the highly hypothetical question: what if the entire management of your company was to die in an airplane crash? If there is something concrete to say, state it ("management never flies together"), otherwise just tell them you are not authorized to speculate on far-fetched scenarios and pick the next question.

You can also get into trouble if someone asks you to do a ranking: which are the best hockey teams in the nation? How would you rank the candidates' comparative intelligence? You can answer ratings questions that are legitimate and safe to answer, otherwise just tell the audience that you really do not have an answer off the top of your head.

You may also face a question based on trying to compare your product or service and another unfairly. You can deal with this one by noting that it is an apples-and-oranges comparison and then restate what is unique about yours ("we are the only union for bartenders in the state park system, so what bartenders earn in major cities is not relevant").

Alert

If someone asks a question that is particularly provocative, but you do have a solid answer, start by saying, "That is an especially good question." The compliment should lower tension surrounding your answer. But if you just say, "That's a good question," this implies the other questions were not good.

If someone wants to rant about a pet peeve, the host should break in to ask what the question is. Or you can interrupt to thank him for sharing the information, but note that others in the audience need to be given time to participate.

If a member of the audience challenges your credentials, you should be prepared to calmly take the opportunity to tell the audience something it did not already know about your background. The introduction may have mentioned your degree, but did not say that you worked up from mail room to management in the industry and have an insider's understanding of it based on hands-on experience. Or you may have written articles for a professional journal. Or you became interested in the disease you are talking about when your mother fell ill and you interviewed top specialists in the field to find out about cutting-edge therapies.

Do not get down and dirty in a serious argument. If your speech did not convince the skeptic, no Q&A exchange is going to do it. Just restate the main reasons you hold to your position and move to the next question. Treat each questioner with dignity. Never attack anyone and never embarrass him, even if he tries to do it to you. Stay centered and you will impress the audience with your self-confidence.

Hecklers

Hecklers have one goal: they want to get you to overreact, make a fool of yourself, and break the rhythm of your speech. Let them spew their venom for a few moments and then tell them that you can address their concerns when you take questions later, along with those from everyone else. That will also buy time for you to think of how you want to respond during Q&A. If the heckler stops at that point, when you come to the end of your talk, you can rephrase his question and answer it in a way that suits you. If he does not accept that answer, you can give him one follow-up question to let him get it off his chest, answer it as best you can, then tell him that others in the audience deserve to have a chance to ask questions, and that you will be happy to talk with him afterward.

 **E** *ssential*

Be prepared with some barbed jokes in case you have hecklers. Focus on the most controversial points in your presentations, the issues where you get the most arguments. A well-developed sense of humor will make you seem cool, throw the heckler off balance, and allow you to continue your presentation.

If the heckler continues to actually interrupt the speech and there is no host to intervene, ask the audience to raise their hands if they would rather have you finish your speech, instead of listening to him for the rest of the period. That should do the trick. If the heckler appears to be drunk, give him one warning that he will have to behave himself or you will call security.

CHAPTER 8

Visual and Audio Aids

Certainly, the key points in your speech are more likely to be remembered if you can underscore the points with audio-visuals (A-V). Some of these are very low-tech and therefore can be used pretty much anywhere—chalk in a classroom, an audiocassette played over a portable tape recorder. Others require training and an entire system of support—making and playing a video or using Microsoft's PowerPoint presentation software. Always have a backup plan, in case your first choice does not work.

Handouts

Regardless of what other type of A-V assistance you use, you should prepare a handout for the audience to take home. If you pass it out in advance, however, some will get distracted from listening to you as they flip through it. Give it out during the question period, if you have one. Otherwise, have assistants hand them out at the exits or make them available on a table to take. Mention this at the start of your speech, so that the audience will not have to frantically scribble notes unnecessarily.

Bring 15 percent more copies of the handout than you think you will need, in case attendance is greater than anticipated. If you do run out, post it on your Web site or give out your e-mail address and ask those who did not get one to send a request or give you their card.

Do not simply make the handout a copy of your slides, which won't tell the audience much because they have few words (more on this in a moment). Provide a written version of everything you mentioned in the speech, at least a detailed outline, including charts and footnotes for support.

Add a Sound Track

A great way to capture the audience's attention is with an audiotape or CD. You might need to wake them up, after some dull prior speeches, with the opening chords of Beethoven's Fifth Symphony as you walk on stage. Or, if you want to put the crowd into an inspired mood, end your talk with a piece that is uplifting.

Alert

There are lots of audiotapes and CDs available for rental or purchase, ranging from the speeches of Martin Luther King Jr. to radio jingles. But paid speakers especially should ask for permission from copyright holders and may have to pay a performance fee for contemporary songs, for example.

Props

Props can stimulate an audience to pay closer attention because they are so rarely used. You may want to hold up a scale model of a proposed building that would be otherwise harder to visualize, or show a photograph of the building as it has been so far constructed, or a map with the route that Alexander the Great's army marched, or a bat that Babe Ruth used.

Props can make a big impact. For example, President Ronald Reagan once held up an enormous stack of paperwork about a proposed budget. He then theatrically dropped it to the floor and declared he would not approve such a budget.

Blackboards, Whiteboards, and Flip Charts

The orators of ancient Greece and Rome and American presidents Abraham Lincoln and John F. Kennedy had little more than voice and body language to help them, and they seem to have done just fine. But if you can better explain information with graphics, then the easiest to use are erasable blackboards or whiteboards and flip charts (pads of paper on easels).

E ssential

If you need to write on the board/chart, stand to the right of it as you face the audience if you are right-handed, or vice versa if you are left-handed, so that you will only partially block it when you write. If you will only be pointing, you can do that from either side.

Ideally, blackboards should be prepared in advance of the lecture, especially if you need to do any drawing that has to be accurate and may take some time. Try to hide what you have written or drawn until you need to show it, lest it distract your listeners. And be sure that there is adequate chalk and an eraser on hand.

The rules for whiteboards and flip charts are similar. The key things to remember for optimum use:

- Use black, blue, green, and red markers (be sure to have extras).
- Write legibly or get help.
- Only write on the top two-thirds of the paper, to be sure everyone in the back rows can see your points.
- The main limit to using flip charts and whiteboards is the size of the audience, so make letters as tall and thick as is appropriate. A letter that is 1½ inches tall and reasonably thick can be seen well enough at about thirty feet.

Although one of the advantages to using flip charts is that you can keep using them over and over, do not hesitate to change anything on the spot, if you discover that a point is not clear to the audience or is effectively challenged. If you do not mind redrawing simple charts, you can also make them more dynamic by adding words, arrows, or underlining as you talk.

Alert

Be sure the easel has been set up in advance and is the right height to allow the pages to be seen in the last row. Some easels can be a little tricky to put together quickly if you have not used them before.

You can also use blank pages to get the audience to participate, such as to brainstorm ideas for promoting a new product or to think of possible solutions to a problem. In this respect, it is more interactive than other visual aids.

Overheads

As long as you have an electrical outlet and the right equipment, overhead transparencies are a simple way to add a little tech to your presentation. The order of presentation can be quickly changed should you decide to take your speech in a different direction after talking with members of the audience before you start or as you present. Transparencies can be seen by a large crowd. And you can add notes to the edges to remind you what needs to be said in the narration.

Compared with slides, videos, and software presentations, overhead projectors are readily available. They can also be shown in fully lighted halls, so you do not risk having to turn lights down and have people doze. And you can mark up transparencies during the presentation to emphasize points or in response to questions. However, they often cannot be seen as well in the back of a large room, so ask in advance about the dimensions of the screen and room.

 Fact

Because overheads are static, you might think they have less ability to convey the information effectively to audiences. In fact, despite the drive for ever-more sophisticated presentation technology, studies have shown that there is no less learning advantage to using overhead transparencies compared with 35mm slides or PowerPoint.

Use a white piece of paper to mask the writing on transparencies before you talk about each line, lest the audience read the whole sheet while you are still narrating the first point.

Slides

Traditional 35mm slides can jazz up a presentation. They are as easy to shuffle as overheads. Slides also have some advantages as support for a speech compared with software presentation programs:

- Slides can be easily carried anywhere in a small box at little risk.
- Unlike having to bring computers and arrange a compatible LCD projector, slide projectors are all the same and available almost everywhere.
- Because slides are less high-tech than presentation software, the audience is less likely to be distracted from the message by special effects.

Of course, slides also do not have the flexibility and creative potential that software programs do, such as the ability to insert film clips.

Standard Videos

Playing a video in the middle of your speech can provide a refreshing break to regain the attention of the audience. They can also be used to bring into the presentation an outside speaker to confirm your message, such as a customer providing a testimonial. An enormous number of video options are available from school and public libraries and commercially. These require either a VCR or a CD-ROM player and a monitor, which are readily available either from the hotel where the speech is taking place, the hosting group, or a local A-V store. However, unless you place multiple monitors around the hall, you will have a limit as to how large an audience can readily see the video (also check that the audio can be heard clearly everywhere in the room).

Alert

Never assume any technology will work! Get to the lecture hall early and check electrical outlets, cord length, the remote control device, microphone, laptop and projector, and Internet connection, if required. Bring extension cords and extra bulbs.

Remember that you are not supposed to be showing any ads or motion pictures without permission, especially if you are being paid to speak. These are copyrighted and companies do not take kindly to having you use their creative work for your personal benefit. Fortunately, there are sources for royalty-free film clips (more on this later).

Of course, you can create your own videos, but only if you either can keep it simple or if you have experience or training to create a professional-level quality.

PowerPoint

Some 400 million people on the planet have access to putting together slide shows using Microsoft PowerPoint (part of its Office suite of programs). Apple also has its own presentation software, Keynote. PowerPoint's popularity has become something of a challenge for speakers, since every audience has already seen its formats, tricks, and graphics too many times. To overcome the jaded effect this can induce and to make it support your message better, there are many things you can do.

First, for those unfamiliar with it, a very basic guided tour of how PowerPoint helps users put together a slide show.

 Fact

PowerPoint's general approach to constructing presentation has not changed greatly over the years, but system requirements have. The still-popular 2000 version only requires a Pentium 75-MHz processor, Windows 95 or later operating system, 20 MB of RAM, and 142 MB of available hard-drive space. The 2007 version needs a 500 MHz processor, Windows XP with Service Pack 2 or Vista, 256 MB RAM, and 1 GB of hard drive.

How It Works

When you open PowerPoint, you are given a choice of three ways to design: using the AutoContent Wizard, a Design Template, or Blank, for an original approach (or you can open an existing presentation for revision). If you click the Wizard, you can choose from general types of presentations (sales, corporate, projects, business plan, financial overview, Carnegie Coach). Then you select from two dozen objectives, including creating a business plan, motivating a team, selling a product or service, communicating bad news, and reporting on the status of a project. Whatever you choose will result in an outline on the left side of the screen with general points you may want to cover.

You also need to pick the type of output you will need for the presentation (on-screen, Web, black-and-white overhead, color overhead, 35mm slides). The Wizard decides on a color scheme, which you can alter.

The familiar Windows toolbars are at the top: Standard (File, Edit, View, Insert, etc.) and Common Tasks (icons for printing, clipboard, bold, etc.). At the bottom is a Drawing toolbar (line color, text box, font color, etc.).

View will allow you to look at the slides in different ways: Normal (one at a time), Slide Sorter (shows a miniature view of each one on a page and allows you to click them to make changes), Notes (to add reminders about what you want to say about each slide, which can also be printed for the handout), and Slide Show (when you want to see how the presentation will look when you switch on the graphics; or you can click Miniature to see a small copy of each slide in the corner of the screen as you work).

E ssential

You can turn a slide show into a black-and-white version for using with an overhead projector and for printing noncolor handouts, using grayscale shading to indicate color differences. In a pinch, like laptop-projector incompatibility or a plug or electricity problem, you could use the handout as a reference for your speech.

The Master option allows you to set the text style for headlines and bullet points on slides, notes, and handouts.

As you move along with the slides, the Insert tool allows you to drop in clip art, photos, movie and sound clips, charts, and Web links.

Slide Show will also allow you to add "animation" effects, determine the time the slide will remain on the screen, and choose a style of transition between slides.

Improving General Design

There are a lot of criticisms of PowerPoint, both because of the options it offers and the fact that everyone has already seen its effects. Below are some problems and how to solve them.

TEMPLATES

PowerPoint's templates give the audience the impression that you are giving a cookie-cutter presentation. There are many sources of other, better designs at places like *www.powerpointtemplatespro.com*. You can save whatever you choose as a new option on PowerPoint.

BACKGROUND AND TEXT COLOR

A problem with using slide shows in general is the habit of turning out the lights. Soon, the main sound effect is someone snoring. If you are speaking as just one part of a program, you may have no choice, so in that event, use a dark green or blue background (white is hard on the eyes) and yellow or light text.

Better, do not darken the room, and rely on the available ambient light. Then use a light pastel background (burnt sienna, light green, gray, pale yellow, and sandy are especially good) and dark text. Keep the same color scheme throughout your slide show, unless it is long, in which case you should alter slightly for the different sections. If you use too many colors in the presentation, it will look cheap.

About 6 to 10 percent of any audience will be color blind, which usually manifests itself by the inability to clearly distinguish colors in the red and green families. They may just appear to be shades of gray. Red should be avoided, green should only be used as a background.

FONT STYLE AND SIZE

Newspapers, magazines, and books (including this one) typically use what is called serif typeface—letters with little flares at the ends. It helps words to be more easily read on a small-print page, but it works just the opposite on a screen, where resolution is low. Use sans-serif letters instead (from French *sans* "without"). Helvetica is the typeface that is most popular (and it has thirty different font variations), but that also means it is overexposed, so this might be a good reason to choose something else.

Use no more than two fonts in your presentation or it will look gimmicky and will be harder to read. Use upper- and lowercase letters, except for **HEADLINES**, which can be all caps and bold.

You want the entire audience to be able to easily read the slide, of course, so test how clearly words can be seen from as far back as the last row will be from the podium (ask the facility, if your sponsoring organization does not know the size of the room). When you project a slide on the screen, the rule of thumb is that 24-point type will be legible from eight times the height of the screen. So if the screen is three feet high, your last row should be no more than twenty-four feet away, if you are using 24-point. If the room is longer, you need to raise your minimum type size proportionally. Most PowerPoint slideshows use 28- to 34-point type size—the bigger, the better, as long as it still looks attractive.

E ssential

Two of the best typefaces to use together for a PowerPoint presentation are Arial and Verdana, the former for text body and the latter for headlines. They look good together and are available on other computer systems, in case you need to send your slideshow over the Net.

HOW MUCH TEXT

Slides are supposed to support your speech, not replace it. The worst sin in using any slide (or overhead) is to read it verbatim as you speak. The audience can do that faster in their heads and will think you are treating them like idiots. Just put up key words to help them to remember the main points (you can be reminded by using PowerPoint's Notes or 3 × 5 cue cards with key words or an outline of the speech).

Richard Mayer, author of *Multimedia Learning*, has done one of the few studies on the subject of how information is processed by an audience watching a slide presentation. His key counterintuitive finding is that people will *retain less if the same phrases are on the slide as the speaker is saying*. A picture with no or minimal words on the screen accompanied by a spoken explanation works better. Irrelevant images or words on the screen distract from the message. Remember, empty space on the slide is a good thing because otherwise it looks cluttered and is hard for the audience to absorb.

 **Alert**

Proofread carefully! Although PowerPoint has a spelling check, you need to actually read your slides carefully as you create them to avoid embarrassment. Few e-mail programs have this function and we have all gotten used to sending casually written messages full of mistakes. Especially double-check all numbers.

Typically, slides should be up for twenty to thirty seconds to allow the audience time to digest them, but adjust the default time to fit each one. If you need to talk longer, perhaps to make a spontaneous digression, it is best to hit the B key on the laptop to make the screen go black until you finish your comments, otherwise the slide could distract the audience from your message.

VISUAL AND SOUND EFFECTS

PowerPoint provides the ability to do "object builds" that gradually put lines on the screen as you discuss each point. Other "animation" techniques and sound effects can be inserted for slide transitions. All have been overused and too many make a presentation look amateurish. They also call attention to themselves. Using the option to wipe the screen from left to right is okay to use because it is fast, but do not do it for every change of slides or it will bore.

Upgrading Art and Photos

PowerPoint offers all kinds of tools and resources to make a slide presentation more interesting for the eyes and ears. Resist the temptation to overdo it and keep the show simple, yet sophisticated.

CLIP ART

PowerPoint provides a library of art; however, the art is cartoonish, so if you have the time to look for something better, your lecture will stand out. The big issue with using clip art from other sources is that it has to either be explicitly stated to be in the public domain or paid for in some way (such as downloading for a fee). If something is offered free to, say, only schools, ask about commercial licensing.

These sites offer free clip art for use in education that is more sophisticated than PowerPoint's: *www.1clipart.com*; *http://etc.usf.edu/ clipart/index.htm*; and *http://school.discovery.com/clipart*. A source of art that can be used commercially for a small fee is *www.corbis.com*.

 Fact

Instead of art, put in photos of people. The photo-sharing site Flickr.com offers many of its users' pictures for free. Other free photo sources are *www.freefoto.com*, *www.pixelperfectdigital .com*, and *www.stockvault.net/gallery*. For commercial and free images, check out *www.gettyimages.com*. A subscription-based service is *www.hemera.com*.

MOVIE AND SOUND CLIPS

The best part of PowerPoint may be its capability to insert video and sound clips. There is no need to order a VCR or turn on a tape recorder. But remember that you are supposed to get written permission to use copyrighted material. No one is going to arrest you for giving a talk at the noon Rotary meeting, but if you are on a paid speaking tour, you either need to get permission from the copyright holder, use public domain material (a bigger challenge with film and sound clips you may want to use), or create your own material.

Extensive free video clips are available from *www.open-video.org* and *www.archive.org/details/movies*. Microsoft Office, of which PowerPoint is part, offers royalty-free music downloads. Thousands of others can be found at *www.archive.org/details/opensource_audio*.

E *ssential*

Freepath.com is a presentation program that many praise as superior to PowerPoint. It can integrate movies, audio clips, Web sites, Adobe Flash player, PowerPoint slides, even Word and Excel, and it works very well transmitted over the Internet. For schools, *www.superteaching.org* offers a multimedia approach to stimulating the senses of students for maximum learning.

Charts and Graphs

As when using paper versions, PowerPoint charts and graphs need to be readily understood by the audience in a matter of seconds. The natural tendency is to use the three-dimensional effects, on the assumption they are more realistic. In fact, experts have shown that these tend to lead to visual distortions and are less readily grasped than traditional two-dimensional graphs.

The best ways to utilize PowerPoint's graphic options are:

- Bar charts are good for showing comparisons over a period of time (data that might otherwise be displayed in a table, which is difficult to absorb at a glance). You might want to use vertical bars to show sales growth in recent years, for example.
- Horizontal bars or pie charts are typically used to indicate the relative size of things, such as different market components of total revenue.
- Line graphs are best for demonstrating trends.
- Flow charts can be designed to show the parts of a process.
- Organizational charts and diagrams can be easily drawn with the tools.

An incredible resource for PowerPoint users is its user-contributed FAQ *http://pptfaq.com/index.html*, which is twenty-plus printed pages of links to tips, tutorials, and answers to every imaginable question or problem.

Ultimately, the type of audio-visuals you use to support your speech, if any, are a matter of comfort about your ease of use and what you feel you need to achieve your objectives.

CHAPTER 9

It's Debatable

Formal debate is verbal combat in a regulated format. It is intense, often with great stakes, and not for the faint of heart. But the skills it requires would aid anyone with leadership responsibility who needs to sharpen her skills of argumentation and persuasion. And the process of learning how to do it right can be both highly educational and even fun, like an intellectual game.

They're Just Formalities

Unless you are a college debater or a political activist, you may never need to have a formal public argument that has to stick precisely to traditional debate technicalities. However, you may find opportunities to present ideas you are passionate about in a variety of situations. You find yourself leading the charge against dropping sports at your son's school and want to make sure other parents hear your views; or, you feel strongly that certain industry trends are dangerous and want to challenge their perpetuators at a trade show; or, your church is becoming divided over an issue in which you have some expertise and you feel it would be helpful for everyone to hear all sides.

Whether the issue is big or small, providing some rules for the discussion can ensure fairness for participants and help members of the audience reach conclusions. But before the format options are discussed, you will need some of the basic debate terminology.

Talk the Talk

Typically, formal debates will center around a proposition, a statement that takes a strong position. For example: "Resolved, there should be no federal limit on the number of guns one can buy each month." The advocate for the proposition is arguing the affirmative or "for" position and the opponent takes the negative side or "against."

This is also the terminology that is used in the booklets about ballot initiatives state governments send to voters before an election. The proponents make the arguments for the proposition, the opponents criticize those arguments and then elaborate their case, and the proponents close with a response.

Opening arguments for both positions in a live debate are called constructive speeches. The debater who goes second may address some of what has just been said by the opponent, but needs to state his basic argument in favor of his position. Most of the direct response should be saved for the rebuttal, when each side challenges the logic or facts behind the other's statements. Rebuttals only last for a few minutes and need to be laser-focused. In some formats, the debaters can ask questions of each other during the cross-examination period.

If you find yourself getting very upset when you hear viewpoints contrary to your own, then debate is not for you. To succeed at it, you have to be able to understand your opponent's thinking and stay calm during the process of argumentation.

Debate Frameworks

There are numerous ways to debate, but following are the most popular ones, which allow each side an equal chance to make its case. You may want to propose one of these if you are invited to participate in a debate.

Parliamentary
The party in government argues for a proposition and the opposition criticizes this, generally relying more on logic than factual evidence. The style can be more theatrical than in other debate types, and heckling is allowed within limits. If you want to see this in action, tune into the BBC when the House of Commons is in session.

Standard
Standard debates are comprised of two teams of two for each side. This makes it much more likely that all issues will be thoroughly discussed, which is especially helpful for novices, who otherwise could be easily defeated by experienced opponents. Initial presentations are often eight to ten minutes, rebuttals typically half that.

Policy
Also known as cross-examination, or CX, this type of debate relies heavily on researched evidence presented by two teams of two; each team member makes her case and then questions her opposite number. Note taking is encouraged.

Lincoln-Douglas
Named after the famed debates between Abraham Lincoln and Stephen Douglas conducted during the 1858 Senate campaign in Illinois, it features single participants debating ethical issues. The format is similar to policy debates, but each side has a shorter time to make its points (five minutes for constructive speech, three for questioning) and is thus known for rapid-fire argumentation, which relies heavily on persuasive logic.

Political Campaigns

A more flexible framework where there is no proposition, this is often used for candidates and ballot issues. There is a short opening statement by each side, followed by primary arguments and rebuttals, sometimes with questioning of each other by the participants, and a short closing statement. The debaters may flip a coin to determine who goes first (depending on the agreement, the first speaker may also go last). In presidential debates during primaries, with numerous candidates to squeeze into 90–120 minutes, rebuttals may be reduced to one minute.

Less Traditional Formats

The truth is that any structured argument that allows a fair exchange of views is legitimate, so do not feel you have to adhere to traditional formats. Opposing presidential candidates always negotiate the details. These are some other recognized ways to debate:

- **Karl Popper:** Popular in Europe and Asia, this style utilizes teams of three, which research both sides of the proposition, a process which helps develop critical thinking skills. The first two speakers have six minutes, the other four have five minutes each, with three minutes for cross examination after the first four speeches.
- **Moot Court/Mock Trial:** Intellectual competitions at colleges often take a courtroom approach to debating issues.
- **Community Forums:** For most people, the closest they are likely to come to participating in formal debate is the regulated give-and-take at a meeting of the city council or a school board.
- **Panels:** These are so common, so flexible, and can serve such a similar function to debate, they may be the best way to get a soapbox for something you want to talk about. Usually a moderator selects recognized experts, sets a time limit for presentations of five to fifteen minutes, and then the audi-

ence can question them afterward. Panelists can challenge each other in their presentations or during questioning.

- **Online Forums:** Internet-based debates using instant messaging software or posting of comments now allow somewhat moderated arguments with international participation.

Goals

Whatever format you use matters little. The outcome really rests on whether you actually have well-thought-out grounds for taking your position that you can clearly explain and your ability to counter the opposition's statements. Before putting together your evidential basis for your reasoning, do you know what you need to accomplish to win?

In the real world, outside of academic debates, there probably will not be judges, just an audience with varying levels of knowledge of the subject. They may be voters you want to convert to support your candidate or they may be workers in a union discussing the pluses and minuses of a proposed contract. In many cases, you will not know the actual impact you have had at the end of the debate. Even if there is a vote at the beginning and at the end, partisans are unlikely to publicly admit to having changed their minds, although you might dampen their enthusiasm by raising disturbing questions about their positions. All you can do is give the process your best shot. That means keeping a few things in mind, especially within the limitations of a traditional debate structure.

The Affirmative Side

If you have the affirmative and are advocating change, you must show that there is a serious problem that needs to be addressed and that your proposal is the best course to that end. You also need to anticipate how the negative side will criticize your positions and develop effective responses, which take into account the knowledge and attitudes of the audience (it does no good to "win" on intellectual points but persuade no one, which happens all too often).

The Negative Side

If you take the negative position, one way to undermine the affirmative is to question whether the problem is as great as it states. Or, conceding that, you could argue that their proposal for change would either not solve this to the extent they claim or would have such negative side effects that it would not be a good trade-off. It is not necessary to offer an alternative plan, but not offering one would likely convince the undecided that you are simply a naysayer without a solution.

Just the Facts, Ma'am

Solid evidence for your position is the foundation of making good arguments. It is, of course, supposed to be factual, but as often as not the facts are in dispute or you would not be debating. Whenever possible, cite a source that is generally perceived as authoritative and fair in treating controversial issues, such as an encyclopedia or an author with widely acknowledged expertise in the field. Even better: quote someone from the opposing side who concedes the fact you want to use.

Sometimes, though, you may need to rely on a source that is highly biased or not well known, yet it is important to make your case, so explain why it should be taken seriously (it relies on multiple credible eyewitnesses, it is based on a double-blind scientific study, it has a long-recognized track record of truthfulness, etc.).

In any event, you should always double-check the information you want to use by looking at other types of sources. Newspapers and Web sites, especially, all too often cite an article that had an error in it that no one caught when it was first published. The more controversial a source is, the more you should recheck it. Online booksellers that allow buyers to post reviews can be a valuable resource in determining which books hold up well under close scrutiny from different viewpoints.

E ssential

If you want to use a source that militantly argues one position, try to find another source that directly addresses the points made. College professors in the field of interest are useful for finding out which books are the best for each side, since they are well-read, they have written on the subject, are very accessible, and like to be cited as experts.

It's Only Logical

Logic is defined by *Webster's New World Dictionary* as "the science of correct reasoning . . . which describes relationships among propositions in terms of implication, contradiction, contrariety, conversion, etc." There are two types of logical reasoning:

- Induction is reasoning from a particular fact to a general conclusion (all sheep we see are white, so all sheep must be white).
- Deduction is the reverse—reasoning from a general conclusion to a particular fact (all sheep are white and you have a sheep, so it must be white).

Never get personal in debates. No matter how stupid or evil you really think your opponent is, keep the discussion focused on the issues. If you indulge yourself in what are known as *ad hominem* arguments, personal attacks, you will appear to have run out of fact-based arguments, and that will make some undecideds sympathetic to your opponent.

Common Mistakes

A bright debater can sound perfectly logical but, because of either ignorance or blind devotion to his cause, can make unsound arguments. Some common ways to make a case that should be avoided:

- Quoting a famous person who is not an expert in the area under discussion.
- Quoting only a portion of a statement because the full comment or its context do not support the point you want to make.
- Using emotionally charged language to incite the audience and blur the argument (baby killer! fascist!). Sometimes this comes in the form of innuendo—the phrase "there are those who seem to want to take away our liberty" could be interpreted as an allusion to the opponent.
- Citing an experiment or poll that had an inadequate sample.
- Using the results of a survey that used biased questions ("should the candidate who wants to undermine our schools be reelected?").
- Relying on majority opinion—conventional wisdom even among experts is often wrong, so really listen to the points that dissenters raise.
- Circular argument—the conclusion assumes something that has not been proven.
- Red herring—an argument used to prove something that is really irrelevant, usually to distract the audience from the real issues.
- Two wrongs make a right—citing injustices to gain sympathy for one's plans.
- Anecdotal fallacy—overestimating the probability of events because of recent experience.
- Assuming correlation is causation: A came before B, so A caused B ("drug confiscations have come down since our new laws targeting major dealers went into effect, so they must not be selling as much").

- Over-generalization ("gun owners like to kill").
- Straw man—setting up an easy target to knock down, even though the example is not representative of the opponent's actual views.
- Using half-truths—facts that sound better for your position if you withhold relevant information.
- Selective reporting—pointing to successes and not failures.
- Putting a priority on worst-case scenarios, regardless of how improbable.
- Only looking at the short-term effects and ignoring the long-term.
- False choices—making it seem that there is only your way or ruin, even though other plans may be equally viable.
- Asserting your own authority—you have credentials and therefore the audience should assume you are right.

The best way to find out whether the arguments you use rely on improper reasoning is to present them informally to someone who disagrees with the positions you are taking and see how well they stand up to criticism. Better that then to have it happen at the actual debate.

Winning Tactics

A logical, evidence-based attack on your opponent's positions and defense of your own obviously makes sense, but is easier to theorize than execute. You may not have the knowledge or debating skills the other side has or even what appears to be the most defensible position on the issues. Following are some keys to improving your odds of winning.

Avoid Acting Arrogantly
Obvious disdain for your opponent's intellect or disrespect of the sincere beliefs of others will tell your audience that you probably are

too close-minded to notice your own blind spots. Arrogance leads to underestimating your opponent and not preparing adequately. Those who think they walk on water are likely to drown first.

Know Thy Enemy

A good general, boxer, or football player wants to know everything he can about the opposition. Try to get an audio or video of your opponent in a debate or on a panel (professional conferences usually sell these and TV programs sometimes make transcripts available). Even if the subject is not the same, this will give you an idea of his style. Note the strengths and weaknesses: he may be a brilliant orator but only brushes off criticisms.

In politics, one of the side effects of the winner-take-all Electoral College is that red states and blue states rarely understand each other, since there is little local debate of the issues. The best thing you could do to understand the other side is spend some time over there: if you are an Air America fan, listen to Rush Limbaugh; if you read redstate .com daily, spend some time on huffingtonpost.com daily.

Over-research the Important Points

Do not clutter your mind with every fact that is not really critical to your argument. But do study everything you can to glean the most relevant information.

Admit mistakes quickly and move on. President Ford misspoke during his debates with Jimmy Carter in 1976 and claimed that Eastern Europe was not under domination by the Soviet Union. Apparently advised never to admit mistakes, he tried to justify his comment during the rest of the debate and for weeks after. It contributed to his defeat.

Listen Carefully

Do not get so caught up in what you want to say next that you do not hear what your opponent is saying right now. Take notes (and bring two pens).

Use Notes

Put your important points on 3 × 5 cards with sources (and bring blank ones for new ideas). You can then easily shuffle them as the argument and your needs change. Also bring backup material to refer to in case something unexpected comes up.

Improve Your Memory

There is a wide range of resources for upgrading your recall, but practicing with someone else and rehearsing without notes are the most important efforts you can make. Quick retrieval and connections among the material you have stored in your head can provide a decisive edge.

Make Your Presentation Memorable

Colorful or humorous phrases will help. Analogies, highlighting similarities between situations, can stick with the audience. You can say that trying to reform the local school is like trench warfare: you need patience to achieve long-term results when you move two steps forward and then one step back very slowly.

Offense Is the Best Defense

Throw out so many criticisms so fast that your opponent barely has time to write them down, let alone think of responses. It will throw off her planned attack.

Master Timing

Practice with rigorous attention to the time you have for each segment and then watch the clock during the debate. An argument half-made convinces no one.

Practice with a Devil's Advocate

A friend who really does disagree with you or someone from your side who knows the opposition's arguments would be very helpful in honing your skills. Or do a trial run before a small group before the big debate.

E ssential

Ask questions of your opponent and your audience, even if that is not part of the format. The 1980 race between President Jimmy Carter and Ronald Reagan was, polls showed, close, despite the hostages in Iran and high inflation. Then in one debate Reagan asked the audience, "Are you better off than you were four years ago?"

Take Their Arguments to the Logical Extreme

Called *reductio ad absurdum*, this applies a principle to such an extent that its flaws appear. If your opponent were to argue that abortion is truly murder, you could point out that anyone who had one performed should then logically be given the death penalty. Conversely, one could argue that those who assert that only the mother should have any say in the choice whether to abort are encouraging support for infanticide.

Make Sure Your Language Is Clear

Avoid jargon and deploy a vocabulary that everyone in your audience will understand. Also you should not make historical or technical references that will only confuse the average person likely to attend. And avoid making such complicated arguments that few will be able to follow.

Keep Your Cool

If you let your opponent rattle you, you will appear to the audience to lack confidence in your position.

If you expect to have numerous opportunities to debate, you should take a course on the subject of formal argumentation. Good books on the subject are *Logical Self-Defense* by Ralph Johnson and J. Anthony Blair or *Fundamentals of Critical Argumentation* by Douglas Walton.

CHAPTER 10

Taking Care of Business

Everything said about the importance of effective communication is especially true in business. There is a world of difference in the outcome between giving a talk to model car hobbyists and the initial sales presentation to try to land a contract to build a $200 million manufacturing plant. Business settings also require more sales skills for public speaking, more need to speak impromptu, and presentations that need to be delivered by phone, video, or over the Web. You will definitely advance your career if you have the ability to speak articulately in public.

Sales Presentations

The biggest problem with sales pitches is that the salesman is too enamored of the minute details of his product's features. Buying decisions are made based on whether something will solve a problem. Extraneous facts obscure the critical benefits, causing the buyer to feel more time is needed to study the information and the competition. Do not fall in love with excessive information that will overwhelm and confuse the customer. Winning techniques include:

- Be sure you know how much time you have to present and plan to finish sooner, since in a one-on-one setting you may get cut short by a phone call your customer has to take.
- Listen to and watch the customer carefully. Arms folded, leaning back, and a lack of questions are likely indicators

that he is not convinced. Get at the roots of his skepticism. Ask questions to get him to divulge his biggest worries about his company, the products they need, current vendors, and the markets they serve.

- Start by reviewing the customer's goals and how your product helps achieve them in the most cost-effective way that best serves his own customers.
- Exude enthusiasm about your offer—too many presentations sound like they have been given hundreds of times and the sales rep is bored with what he is saying.
- Relate experiences about how customers solved similar problems. Stories make the benefits real and stick in the memory better than simple facts.
- If the customer asks a question, do not simply spout the company line: acknowledge the strengths of competitive products and even the weakness of your own, then show why your total offering will help the customer gain a long-term advantage over his competition.

By far the most important part of a presentation is actually the preparation in advance of giving it. Studies show that the sales cycle can take 20 percent less time if the right homework has been done. Make sure you study a variety of sources to understand the problems and opportunities facing the customer so that you can adjust what you say accordingly.

 Fact

The Carnegie Foundation did a study that found that only 20 percent of a salesperson's success came from product knowledge, the rest came from interpersonal and personal management skills.

One way to make selling easier is for management to listen to feedback the sales rep collects directly from customers and to use that to design the products and marketing. Peter Drucker said, "The aim of marketing is to make selling superfluous . . . to know and understand the customer so well the product or service fits him and sells itself."

Speaking Off-the-Cuff

Sales people are often asked to talk informally without much preparation. For those who may be called upon to speak on the spot, it is best to remember what Mark Twain said: "It takes three weeks to prepare a good ad-lib speech."

Carry around a few quotes from famous people that address common business situations, which you can pull out for impromptu speeches. Good sources for these include *Quotable Business* edited by Louis Boone, *The Quotable Manager* edited by Joel Weiss, and *The Forbes Book of Business Quotations* edited by Ted Goodman.

To prepare to speak "impromptu" eloquently, find out what the subjects and objectives are for upcoming meetings. Make sure you know what is likely to be expected of you, not only in your area of expertise, but in case you are asked to give an opinion about broader company issues.

Do some extra research in your field. Go beyond the first few pages of results for an Internet search. Actually read some of the articles in trade magazines, rather than just glance at the news. Make it a habit to always be reading one of the 3,000 business books published in the United States each year (Harvard Business Press and Amacom especially put out volumes of fresh thinking). Leave it to your brain to synthesize all this material and to come up with something interesting to say at the right moment.

Practice responses to possible questions out loud (thinking about them in your head is never the same). Tape yourself, listen, and keep improving each one.

If you are completely surprised by the topic you are asked to address, buy a few moments to collect your thoughts by restating the question and acknowledging its importance to the company.

E ssential

The "elevator speech" refers to the 100–150 words that can explain why your business proposition should succeed in the thirty seconds an elevator ride might take. It came about during the dot-com explosion, when venture capitalists were overwhelmed by proposals and needed an instant way to judge a prospect. Make sure your elevator speech does not sound too rehearsed, avoids jargon, is simple, and makes sure your unique competitive advantage will be remembered.

And most importantly, do not ramble: give the best couple of points you can come up with, provide brief support, and sit down. No one will expect you to be Churchill on a moment's notice.

A Numbers Game

Numbers and statistics usually bore people, but they are often necessary to use in business presentations. Your speech is not a press release, so let the audience consult one if they want the details. Your goal is to give the numbers meaning, so that their implications are better understood and remembered. One way is to provide the long-term view. A 3 percent annual growth rate may not sound impressive, but show how that compounds over ten or twenty years and what the difference would be if it were just 2 percent.

Or give the numbers relevance to daily work by linking small contributions to the company to the total. Show that success came by making a few more sales calls per day or by answering customer service questions sent to the Web site in half the prior time.

Or look at the bigger picture. The potential for a medicine may not be appreciated if you just look at the incidence of a disease in the United States instead of the entire world. Allowing employees to take off more personal time could be seen as a loss of work time, or you could cite the results of a survey of the greater work satisfaction and loyalty among those who were allowed more personal time.

 **Alert**

Be sure to cite the source of your numbers so that members of the audience do not wonder if they are credible. Read numbers slowly, so that listeners have time to absorb them. Repeat the most important ones. Round numbers off to make them simpler to grasp.

Or you could make comparisons. There were 58,000 American military deaths during the Vietnam War, when the population of the United States was 212 million, which is 1 out of 3,655. There were 620,000 deaths on both sides during the American Civil War when the combined population of the United States and Confederacy was 32 million, or 1 out of 52.

Or you could relate an anecdote that puts the numbers into perspective or relates them to daily life. If your company is trying to create new malaria medicines, note that the disease threatens half of the world's population, yet the National Institutes of Health spent less than one-third of 1 percent of its budget on malaria research. Then tell the story of a family that is alive today because of your experimental medicine.

International Audiences

By now, globalization should have dispelled the illusion that American business does not need to cater to other cultures. Almost inevitably, all but the smallest companies (and even those, if they have Web sites) will start to have customers or suppliers in other countries. E-mail, airmail, telephones, and even video-streaming over the Net have some limitations that may only be lifted by meeting with buyers or vendors in person.

If you have the opportunity to make a presentation in another country, find out as much as you can about cultural differences. If your company has an international branch, talk with Americans who have lived over there long enough to make a full transition and understand the subtleties of speaking etiquette. Employees who have immigrated to the United States will also be helpful. Other resources could be business associates from that country, friends at your synagogue/ church, university professors, the nation's consulate, the library, and the Internet (searching on "cultural differences U.S. Philippines" gets 1.3 million results). Or look at the cultural tips in most travel guides.

 Fact

Perhaps the most famous example of lack of thorough preparation for saying something in public in another language was President John F. Kennedy's statement in Berlin in 1963, "Ich bin ein Berliner," which literally means, "I am a Berlin-style pastry." To indicate that he felt solidarity with the residents, he should have said, "Ich bin Berliner."

When speaking, a few things will help make it more likely that a foreign audience understands what you are trying to communicate:

- Keep it simple.
- Avoid idioms (phrases that are not meant to be translated literally like "he'll do it in nothing flat," "she's a smart cookie," or "it's selling like hotcakes").
- Avoid industry jargon that is not internationally understood.
- Quote someone from that country on the subject.
- Use a local anecdote or case study.
- Say something about the relationship between your countries and their shared values and interests.
- Keep it short and talk at a moderate rate, especially if you are being translated live.
- Provide handouts with the most important information from your presentation.

Even doing business in the same language can present communication challenges. As Oscar Wilde said, "We have really everything in common with America nowadays, except, of course, language." Find out the local lingo for English words that may differ in the other culture.

Be sure to have someone from that country read over your speech to be sure there is nothing that will be misunderstood or not a good cultural fit. If you use an interpreter, try to get someone who is a native speaker who also knows your industry.

Speaking in Tongues

It is dangerously naive to think that the best way to conduct global business is to insist that everyone you do business with in other countries learn your language, while you do not learn theirs. This makes you entirely reliant on a translator, perhaps one supplied by your hosts, assuming one is available at all. Otherwise, when it comes to understanding them, you will only know what they want you to know.

Even if you are going to give a speech in English to a foreign audience, you should know some phrases in the other language to open and close the presentation, and perhaps a few words to put here or there in between. The audience will appreciate the effort and you will build rapport. They may wonder how much you really know, and this could limit their candid discussions with each other during negotiations, which would be good for you.

E ssential

A 2002 survey by the Modern Language Association found that just 8.6 percent of college students were enrolled in a foreign language course. Of the 1.3 million learning another language, 746,000 were studying Spanish and 202,000 were in French classes. Japanese was the subject for 52,000, while 34,000 were studying Chinese and 24,000 were taking Russian, with less than 11,000 learning Arabic.

If you can learn even a little of another language, it will also help you understand the way people think in that culture.

Today, advancements in language teaching have made learning conversational basics much easier than ever before. The easiest way is to take an "immersion" class for a few months, in which the new language is all you are allowed to speak. You can also take this approach in a less effective piecemeal form several times a week at most major language-training schools.

Other super-speedy language-teaching methods have been developed by Super-Learners of Beverly Hills, the Michel Thomas Language Centers, the Rosetta Stone company, Power-Glide Foreign Language Courses, Pimsleur Language Programs, and others, most of which have their courses on CD and audiotape.

Virtual Meetings

After September 11, 2001, the hassles of travel and the impact of rising fuel prices made it attractive to do more business meetings and presentations by telephone, videoconference, and the rapidly improving technology of the Internet.

Teleconferencing

One survey reported that only 22 percent of teleconference participants thought their meetings were productive. If you are going to make a formal presentation by phone or be an active respondent, you need to pay some attention to the basics of putting together a telephone meeting to maximize success. These include:

- Increase attendance by scheduling at a convenient time for all time zones and making sure notifications go out as far in advance as possible, with a reminder the day before.
- Arrive early to be sure the equipment is working properly.
- Consider using a wired phone with headsets that have the microphone in front of the mouth, for improved sound quality over speakerphones (do not use cordless or cell phones and turn off call waiting, usually by pushing *70). If you do use speakerphones have participants turn off their mute button until someone wants to speak, to avoid picking up background sounds.

Other tips include:

- Turn off cell phones, beepers, and watch alarms.
- Ask everyone to call in two minutes before the start time and remind them that they should identify themselves when they speak.
- Do not wait more than five minutes to start, and have a firm time to end; otherwise you may lose those that have other things to attend to after the call.

- Send out an agenda and stick to it.
- Send materials to be referred to during the teleconference by mail or e-mail in advance.
- Leave substantial time for discussion after the presentation.
- Speak clearly.
- At the end, recap action items, then send out a summary of decisions within twenty-four hours.
- Tape-record the conference, in case there are disputes about what was said. You may want to even send out the transcript.

 Fact

A telephone bridge works like conference calling, but without using a commercial conference service with an operator, thus lowering the cost. These are widely available—just google "telephone bridge" for providers.

Videoconferencing

Large companies may have permanent videoconferencing rooms at major locations, equipped with very high-quality equipment produced by companies like Polycom and Sony. These are effective not only for internal company meetings, but also for training (as well as communicating with customers who either have their own video facilities or come in to the supplier's conference room).

The tips for teleconferencing apply to videoconferencing as well:

- Have the rooms brightly and evenly lit.
- Test the equipment and have presenters work with it in advance.
- Make sure that everyone who is going to speak can be seen and heard and remind them to look at the camera.

- Avoid excessive movements (such as swiveling in your chair), which can be distracting to viewers.
- Wear blue or black and avoid bright white, red, or excessively patterned clothing, as well as large or noisy jewelry (see the section on TV appearances in Chapter 12).
- Check your appearance before you go on the air.
- Use large fonts and pictures for presentation materials (see Chapter 8).

You will probably want to record the conference for future reference. Let everyone know this is being done.

Alert

It is easy to forget that everyone can see everyone else. Ask that no one look at their e-mail or incoming cell calls during the discussion, since this would not only be obviously impolite, but would make it clear that this person is not very interested in the objectives of the meeting.

Web Conferencing

The video-streaming technology of the Net has so rapidly advanced that sites like YouTube have become part of popular culture almost overnight. All one needs is a high-speed connection, a webcam, and the software or use of a site for transmission, making desktop videoconferences and training sessions feasible. That said, the technology is still evolving and quality varies a lot.

The industry leader in Web conferencing and teaching seminars (known as webinars) is WebEx. Other popular hosts are GoToMeeting and Megameeting.com (which claims to offer the most simultaneous video windows so that up to sixteen participants can be seen).

These technologies also allow presenters to show PowerPoint or other materials.

Many videoconferencing services charge a lot per month. However, you can add streaming user-friendly video and video chat to a Web site for a one-time fee using *www.camfrogweb.com*.

 Fact

Wainhouse Research found, in one survey of 116 users of video-conferencing, that generating sales leads was the number one goal and they generated 32 percent more leads this way than through traditional events. Webinars were also used for internal and external training, company announcements, and communicating with partners and customers.

Some recommendations for optimizing Web meetings, in addition to what has been said about teleconferences and videoconferences, include:

- Be sure everyone has log-in information and passwords.
- Focus the webcam and be sure that you are centered on the screen.
- Remove anything in the background that might be embarrassing (like a poster or, if you are at home, a pile of laundry).
- Be sure you are not sitting in front of an open window that will light you from behind and put you in a shadow.
- Most Web software has a free trial, so take a test run so that you are familiar with how it works.
- Ask the audience questions during the presentation to stimulate interaction (it is easy to zone out in front of a screen).
- If you have asked the audience to submit questions, they need to be prioritized in advance to decide what to address first, or, if the audience is big and questions can be submitted

by e-mail live, you may want to have someone with experience sort them as they come in.

- If you want to demonstrate an application, be sure everyone's software will support it. Keep designs simple to speed display.

You may want to hire a professional moderator for an important Web conference, to be sure everything runs smoothly.

Working with a Speechwriter

You may be quite a capable speaker, but not a particularly clear writer. Or your career responsibilities may be so heavy that the last thing you want to do in your free time is to try to come up with inspiring words for a special occasion. You cannot simply turn over the task to someone who knows your style and is a good manager of some aspect of the business but not an experienced writer of speeches. In short, you may want to hire a speechwriter for an important event.

Never circulate an outline of a speech or a first draft to a large number of senior executives for comment. You will end up with the proverbial camel designed by committee or end up offending those whose advice you do not take. Instead, ask department heads to submit the most important points or news to touch on, then show the draft to a couple of trusted advisors.

The first challenge would be to find the right person. The best and quickest way would be to recall a speech you liked and ask the speaker if she can refer you. Otherwise, just send out an e-mail to your electronic Rolodex and you will probably get several recommendations. Or check ads in the local business journal (including classifieds). You can also call the local chapter of the International Association of Business Communicators at *www.iabc.com* or post a job at its Web site. If your company has a public relations firm, they probably have worked with a freelance speechwriter. In the event you still come up empty, google "hiring speechwriter" for some ideas (you can add your city to the search, but the truth is that a pro can collaborate quite well just using the phone and e-mail).

E *ssential*

Check your ego at the door. If you have never worked with a professional speechwriter, this may be the first time you will be getting a real critique of your speaking style. Make it clear that you do not want a yes-man who will tell you that all your proposed changes are fabulous and you are reading the result perfectly.

Some other public-speaking books recommend a long list of questions to be asked before you hire a speechwriter. That probably will not get you much closer to the ideal than the essential questions. If you did not find the writer through a recommendation, ask him for some references, ideally someone he has worked with more than once (if you can find a client he served on a tight deadline or who had a particularly demanding audience, all the better). Ask the reference for a sample speech she gave and to state off-the-record at least one weakness of the writer.

Ask the writer to give you the nearest example of his work for the type of speech you are going to give. This does not mean it has to have anything to do with the particular subject. You may be in the cement business and the speech you are shown may have been delivered to financial advisors, but if customer service was the theme, it should give you a sense of relevant content and style. Ask for a second sample that has nothing to do with your subject but that will show you how flexible the writer's style is in capturing different voices. If the writer has a problem giving you entire speeches because they belong to clients, he can still show you excerpts.

Another approach to vetting the right writer would be to pay him to suggest improvements to a couple of your prior speeches (only a desperate non-pro would do this for free, knowing that he may be just one of many candidates in a very preliminary process and that a critique that will impress you will take some time).

Expect to pay $50 to $100 or more per minute of the proposed speech length. Alternatively, *Writer's Market* says payment per hour ranges from $43 to $167, including researching, interviewing, and doing revisions. If interviewing others for input is necessary, that will add to the final bill.

 **Alert**

Do not have the writer depend on written speeches to get your voice: interviews with you are also important.

Ask for an estimated time for getting the first draft and be sure both of you will have time for follow-up work before the day it has to be delivered. The earlier in the process you can start working with the speechwriter, the better the result is likely to be and the less it will likely cost.

If you want to have the writer turn the speech into a visual presentation, like PowerPoint, you will be charged much more. The most helpful element of a speech the writer can get is a story—or multiple anecdotes that illustrate the points you want to make. This usually takes brainstorming to recall the best examples, so prepare to give this real thought, not just offer the first things that come to mind.

Make sure the main objective of the speech does not get lost in the frills: stories that are not entirely on point, jokes, cute phrases, quotes from great minds, alliteration. You want the audience to remember your message long after they heard you.

CHAPTER 11

Media Interviews: Preparation

Speakers often think too big or too small about how to achieve their goals. Nowhere is this more important than when you are to be interviewed by the media or have your speech recorded for broadcast. If you do not think big enough, you will not do the necessary preparation to get the maximum possible coverage of your message. On the other hand, if you do not pay attention to the smallest detail, any mistake can be magnified millions of times over.

Media Relations 101

Very few people are prepared to speak with journalists during a crisis: a charity whose board you sit on falls far short of its fundraising goals; the rabbi resigns over religious disagreements with your congregation and you are the spokesperson; the division you manage loses a major customer. At that point, reporters may be hounding you and you may not have all the information you need to properly respond. In order to talk to the media effectively, you need to understand some basics about journalism and publicity, as well as develop a strategic process that starts long before you might be in the limelight. Even if you have a corporate PR person to drum up interest in what you say or you are speaking at an organization's convention, you should have an entrepreneurial attitude about making sure as many as possible will be listening. How would you feel if you flew across the country for a break-out section and only a half dozen people showed up? What if your interview is your only shot at a newspaper audience and you misspeak because you were not prepared for a sticky question?

Journalists

Most reporters and freelance writers do not earn much and often work long hours under high pressure, so why do they stay in the profession? Many of them have an insatiable appetite for interesting information and they want to use it to write articles or broadcast pieces that will influence the world for the better. They need inherent drama in a story and a news hook or angle that has not been over-reported so that their editors will assign it right now. Drama tied to current events will also help snag the attention of the audience.

 **Alert**

> Never pitch the same story idea to directly competing media at the same time. No reporter wants to put time into something that could be scooped by a competitor. Most magazines will not do an in-depth profile of someone written up in a competing publication in the past year or more, unless there is a strong news hook that significantly changes the story.

While the rule is that press releases should be distributed to all media at the same time, you can offer advance notice and an interview to one preferred outlet, on condition that the story will be embargoed until the news appears on the wires.

Reporters also have a fear of being naive about a subject they know little about when they write a story, lest they get manipulated by the source, so prepare for them to be skeptical about what you claim. Journalists tend to have a populist streak and sympathy for the underdog, so if you are a well-established organization or business, you may feel the initial questions are hostile or suspicious. Respond to every press query quickly and give the writer more than he asks for well before the deadline and you will be going a long way to establishing credibility that can be very helpful if you face a crisis.

Build long-term relationships by helping journalists, such as providing sources for stories listed on their editorial calendars (many can be found at *www.myedcals.com*, but otherwise ask what they will be working on over the next six months).

Also, do not overlook freelance writers, who may already have relationships with the publications you want to get into. They can be found through the American Society of Journalists and Authors at *www.asja.org*, the Writers Union at *www.nwu.org*, and Authors Guild at *www.authorsguild.org*.

Research the work of journalists you are pitching story ideas to in order to understand their views and approach to issues.

E ssential

Googling a writer's name will yield a lot of irrelevant references, but you should check out at least the first few pages. Also consult the newspaper or magazine's own archive, if it is searchable online, otherwise visit the publication or a library for back issues or microfilm copies. Even better, subscribe to what media professionals use, LexisNexis or PR Newswire's MediaAtlas.

After you send an e-mailed or mailed proposal, you can call to find out what the status is and determine the journalist's preferred means and frequency of contact. If your idea gets rejected, do not take it personally—the final decision was probably not his and reporters are pitched far more ideas than they can cover. Move on to your second choice and if that does not get a positive response, perhaps you need to rethink the news hook and angle.

Publicists

Harold Burson, founder of Burson-Marsteller, the world's largest public relations agency, says companies should not think of a PR agency primarily as something to send out press releases, but as a resource for strategic counsel on how to do the right thing and get credit for it. Ideally, you would have both an internal publicist and an outside agency to handle PR needs, since it is a labor-intensive process that is highly reliant for success on established relationships. You can find publicists (ideally, they would be ex-journalists) through your local Yellow Pages, the Public Relations Society of America at *www.prsa.org*, the Council of Public Relations Firms at *www.prfirms.org*, or the International Association of Business Communicators at *www.iabc.com*.

E ssential

Guerrilla Publicity by Jay Levinson, Rick Frishman, and Jill Lublin is the best handbook for do-it-yourself PR. They point out that the best campaigns start nine months before an event takes place and require tremendous patience in cultivating reporters. You can also generate media interest by listing yourself as an expert on any number of subjects at *www.profnet.com* or *www.expertclick.com*.

Having PR counsel on retainer saves money, but most small businesses (or perhaps you are the lone crusader for a local cause) cannot afford even a freelance publicist for a project ($100 an hour versus $150–$300 for an agency). The alternative is to slowly master the most important details of successful PR.

Whatever you spend on publicity, though, coverage by the press is much more credible and effective in getting your message out than advertising. To locate 70,000 media outlets in North America, consult *www.mediafinder.com*. If you are a business, trade magazines will likely be very receptive to well-thought-out proposals for interviewing executives, covering speeches, or showing up at press conferences.

Your Audience

The old philosophical question asks, "If a tree fell in the woods and no one was around, would it make a sound?" If you apply the question to your speech, the answer is no: you would not want to bother giving one if you knew no one would attend. The press can help deliver the public to hear your message. Likewise, you want to be sure that if you are interviewed, your words will reach your intended audience. To be effective, you need to think carefully about who would be interested in your message, what your objectives are in reaching them, and how best to go about doing this.

Prioritize the outlets that are most likely to offer the biggest bang per buck of your time. Often, that means starting small: it is likely to be a waste of time trying to get on *Oprah*, but a local talk show would be excited to have you as a guest. No one from *Vanity Fair* will respond to your pitch letter, but the local city magazine will.

 **Alert**

Do not overlook weeklies, "alternative" publications, college newspapers, public access TV and radio, special interest magazines, local business publications, ethnic newspapers, and relevant Web sites.

Overwhelmed by the size of a good media relations program? If you have not directly engaged in courting the press before, that is a natural reaction. If you cannot get some help—even other volunteers—relax. Slow, persistent, and informed pursuit of properly prioritized goals should eventually yield results. It can take months or over a year for even a PR professional to get an interview commitment from the major media (which is why PR agencies charge a lot when they are paid only when they place an article and why it is much more cost-effective in the long run to put a publicist on retainer).

Press Releases

Half the ideas that the media decide to cover come from proposals from outside the newsroom. Most of those will be due to a reporter seeing a press release and calling for more information before they are even pitched a story angle on the news. They see so many releases, though, yours must follow certain rules to have any chance of getting their attention.

E ssential

A media alert advises the press of an event that they can cover, preferably a week in advance, with a reminder the day before. It should be sent out in a bare-facts format that answers what the event is about, where it will take place, what the schedule will be, who will be speaking, and why the public should be interested.

Headline

This is likely to be the only part that a harried reporter will read, unless it demands closer attention. That comes from a one-line headline that is interesting, newsy, and cleverly worded. Another subheadline can add a little more detail to motivate the reporter to read the first paragraph. Keeping in mind the public's obsession with health, sex, and money, examples might be:

- Company's Product Beats Cancer—New Study Shows Promising Results

- Women Open Adult Store Aimed at Couples
- Hot Local Stock—Inventor Takes Company Public

If your subject is more mundane, no need to worry. Just have everyone around you brainstorm titles for a couple of days and you will get more ideas than you can use. You can also put a few bulleted subheads at the top to increase interest.

The Body

What are your goals with the release? Do you want to sell something, publicize an event, get recognition for an award, or change your organization's image? Is your real audience the media or are you hoping they will pick it up to pass on to the ultimate consumer? If you can make this important to the broadest audience possible, that will attract more media attention. The first paragraph needs to keep the objectives in mind and explain the purpose for the release clearly in a few sentences.

The next paragraphs should provide more detail about why the subject of the release is important or relevant right now. The news hook may just be something like a new waterproofing product just before the rainy season or a horror movie to be released before Halloween. Include a quote from one or two key people involved, with titles.

Double-spaced on letterhead, the release should not be more than two pages. If you have more detail you think is really important, put it into an accompanying fact sheet or refer to a supporting document on your Web site.

"Boilerplate" is the last paragraph: a summary description of your organization that explains exactly what it is your organization does and why it is significant. Perhaps the group is advocating space tourism and is headed by a former astronaut. Or you are the world's biggest widget maker. Do not assume the reader of the press release already knows anything, no matter how big your company is or that your charity has been around for a century. Reporters' beats can change and the new one assigned to you may be surprisingly uninformed on even the basics (the assumption of the editor is that she will come up to speed quickly with the help of people like you).

E ssential

In response to interest stimulated by a press release, send a media kit that is truly relevant. If this is for a reporter who is just writing background for your news, do not send everything but the kitchen sink. For a business profile, you could include prior articles written about the company and 10-Ks and -Qs if the company is public.

Basic contact information will be on your stationery, but give the name of one or, even better, two people with their cell phone numbers and e-mail addresses. The contacts should be available in the hours following a release and should check their messages frequently. If a significant reaction is expected, whoever is going to be the person to be interviewed must clear her schedule that day in order to allow reporters to meet their deadlines. If the first choice is not available, offer a backup source to answer questions.

Distribution

Most press releases from U.S. companies are distributed via either Business Wire or PR Newswire (from which AP and other syndicated wire services rewrite and disseminate their versions of the news). National distribution to PR Newswire's US1 list (4,800 print outlets, over 2,000 TV and radio stations, 3,600 Web sites) costs $680 for 400 words. There are also regional, international, and trade lists available for distribution. Anyone who is willing to pay can use these, not just businesses.

Alternatively, you can distribute to your own list of relevant outlets by fax or e-mail (the smallest of which will probably not be subscribers to the wires, so you will need to do some of this anyway). Or you can use an online alternative like *www.expertclick.com*, *www .internetnewsbureau.com*, or *www.xpresspress.com*.

Alert

Ideally, set up distribution when both you and the reporters you want to reach will be in your offices. If you send out too late in the day, no one will likely see it right away and it may get buried by the next morning's news. Routine financial news for publicly held companies is the exception.

Questions
With all media, it is smart to send a list of suggested questions. Think of every important aspect of your subject and what question would give you the opportunity to talk about it. Print journalists will generally be reading lots of material on your organization and will have a pretty good grasp of the issues. TV will be likely to want you on for a very short time and the questioning is more likely than radio to be polite and superficial. But few radio show hosts will have time to read your book or do more than scan the press kit: they handle a lot of guests and love it when they can seem like experts by asking the questions you provided. You can also encourage them to send a list of other issues they want you to address.

Be sure to include some questions that bring up controversial issues that have been in the press, which will help make the host seem like he is not giving you a free ride, maintaining his image of journalistic integrity. If he does not ask about sensitive issues, someone else may in a way that is less easy to counter.

Prepare for hostile questioning from listeners in advance by practicing with someone who can give you a hard time. Take responsibility for any mistakes your organization has made and talk about what it is doing to solve the problems that have been reported. On the other hand, you do not need to go into excessive detail, which will be more than listeners want to know (instead, refer them to your Web site for more information).

You can also use challenging moments to bridge to your main message, such as, "Despite these setbacks, we now have safeguards in place and I think everyone who knows our company agrees that we have by far the best product and service in the industry."

Always stay calm in the face of criticism; if you get too defensive, you will make listeners think you are unsure of how right you are. Never be too argumentative with a journalist, who can talk about you after you leave or write another article without your cooperation.

CHAPTER 12

Media Interviews: Showtime

B y this point in the process of getting media coverage, you have studied your subject, the audience, and the reporters you may be facing. You have laid the groundwork with media kits, suggested questions, and provided either a press release or some publicity to attract attention to your message. Only now are you ready to open your mouth and step into the limelight. No matter what the medium you are interviewed in the pressure to perform is on. However, your preparation ensures that the risk of a misstep is minimal.

Radio Interviews

Long before the media will want to talk with you, especially for broadcast, you will need to be well prepared in a variety of ways. As with other types of public speaking, practice as much as you can, including taping yourself to be sure you make your points succinctly. Do some research to understand what type of audience you are addressing and listen to the call-ins if you can—some have online archives— and check out Internet chat about the program. Most radio interviews will be done remotely, so you can consult notes as you talk from your office or home. If you go to the station, bring easily read cards with your not-to-be-forgotten points, since things that should be really easy to remember can slip your mind under pressure.

A Memorable Performance

Someone called radio "theater of the mind" and the best results are achieved when you can stimulate the listener to see what you are talking about with her mind's eye. Vocal dynamics, colorful adjectives, vivid metaphors, anecdotes, memorable phrases, and sparing use of numbers are especially important for this medium. Avoid jargon the audience may not understand.

 **Question**

> **What if I don't get any calls?**
> It is not a big deal, since many off-peak-hour talk shows do not expect them. But if you can, have a friend call in to share a related experience or ask a question not on your press list (but only if they can hear the program, since otherwise it may become obvious it is a setup because he does not know what happened during the broadcast).

As media trainer to the stars Joel Roberts (of Joel D. Roberts and Associates in Los Angeles) points out, radio and TV rely on keeping the audience's attention by a back-and-forth conversation between host and guest. It's a tennis match that has to keep moving, so don't give a monologue. Another important quality talk shows look for in guests: strongly held opinions. If you try to offend no one with mushy middle-of-the-road pleasantries, listeners will tune out.

Keep an eye on the clock so that your answers do not go into such detail that the host cuts to a commercial before you can finish your point.

Since listeners may be driving and cannot write anything down, help them recall your organization's name and location or Web site (or ask the station to post it on its Web site and plug that).

On the other hand, many programs want you as a guest not simply to promote your cause or service, but to help the audience, so be clear about how hard you can push: an "infomercial" will alienate the host and the audience.

E ssential

Offer to be interviewed on standby, in case a scheduled guest cancels at the last minute (it does happen). If you are willing to make yourself available 24/7 they will remember that you are their best bet for an emergency. Conversely, if you get bumped, just say you understand and are eager to reschedule anytime.

Sound Bites

A brief, memorable phrase—a sound bite—is the best way for your message to stick in the listeners' minds and stand out from everything else. What you want to do is to summarize your unique offering in a sentence or two, like an ad headline, but you want a number of these to make sure your key points are more likely to be remembered. If you can make your sound bites a little dramatic, fun, or colorful, that will improve the odds of recall. Examples:

- Bob's Classic Autos has been in business almost as long as its vintage cars and we have models you can find nowhere else.
- Lisa's Hypnotherapy Center guarantees that if you listen to our tapes, you will get rid of your bad habits forever. That includes overeating, drinking too much, and smoking.
- If you owe the IRS back taxes on undeclared income, I can cut a deal that will let you sleep soundly again.

As naturalist-philosopher Henry David Thoreau said, "You have to shout loud to make the deaf hear." You should not worry about using hyperbole. Read your sound bites to others and then ask them to repeat them the next day to see what they remember.

TV Interviews

Joel Roberts, the media trainer, reports that many executives who are invited to be on TV think it is better to be taped, rather than live. They are wrong, he says: if you misspeak, you can correct yourself immediately or address the issue in some other way after the program. But when a show is taped, it will be edited and you have no control over what will be used. In the case of expert comments on news, you might talk for five or ten minutes and they use only one sentence.

E *ssential*

"Do not be hasty to praise or blame; speak always as though you were giving testimony before the judgment seat of the gods," advised Seneca the Younger in "De moribus."

Ask if you can bring some small cue cards to put on the desk during the interview, which will help you overcome nerves and remember important points. If this is not allowed, practice visualizing the key words.

Get a Media Coach

Do not assume that because you can speak well from a podium that you will be fine on television. If you expect to be appearing even occasionally on regional or national TV, you definitely need professional training. Look in the Yellow Pages under "Coaches and Communications Consultants" and online for "media training" or "media coaching" to get help. You can learn a lot in a single day or weekend, but more extended work will make you much smoother and more relaxed. Coaches will teach you how to gesture and use facial expressions so that you do not seem so wooden. They can help you boil down your message into thirty-second bursts. And they will make you look better in ways you will not notice if you critique your own video rehearsals.

Alert

> Do not drink coffee before you go on camera because it will make you seem too excited. And do not drink alcohol or take a pill to relax or you will not be able to think quickly enough. Instead, exercise, take deep breaths, or meditate.

Some pointers from T. J. Walker of Media Training Worldwide include the following:

- Do not look at the camera unless there is no host.
- Lean slightly forward or you will look stiff—and it is okay to move a little.
- Nod and tilt your head.
- Smile slightly, even when you are talking.
- Keep your hands above your waist and gesture occasionally, but not above your face, below your chest, or wider than your shoulders.

Makeup and Clothing

Vice President Richard Nixon, running against John F. Kennedy, refused makeup before the first televised presidential debate in history in 1960. What he did not know is that makeup would have closed his pores; instead, he sweated profusely under the camera lights, while JFK appeared cool. He also looked pale, having just gotten over an illness. Radio listeners thought Nixon won, while those who watched the debate believed he lost and the result contributed to his very narrow loss in the election.

Some makeup tips include:

- Do not rely on makeup professionals to do the work you need before going on. There may not be any at the station or they may not have the right makeup or the time to work on you adequately.
- Apply pancake makeup that matches your skin in advance or bring some with you for a professional to use (but do not use too much or you will look chalky).
- A light blush below the eyes can mitigate bags or dark circles.
- Do not use lipstick so bright it will draw too much attention. Ditto for nail polish (but be sure your nails are well groomed, of course; men tend to forget about this).

 **Alert**

If you arrive late for a live broadcast, you are DOA. Assume traffic will be terrible. If you get there early, you will have an opportunity to review your notes right before you go on, build rapport with the interviewer, go over the format, have a sound check, and get made up.

As for clothing, the experts say:

- Blues, grays, brown, camel, and khaki are the best colors for TV. Avoid stripes and patterns that will distract viewers (a striped tie is okay). Do not wear bright white shirts. Too much cleavage will attract viewer attention away from your message.
- Men need to wear long socks if viewers will see their legs, while women should not wear dark hosiery.
- Keep jewelry to a minimum, nothing too gaudy or jangling.

- Contact lenses are best, although glasses can be worn. Get glare-proof lenses or tilt the glasses slightly forward to keep them from reflecting.

Study how guests appear on any program and you will get a better idea how to dress for TV success.

Print Interviews

Provide a fuller press kit to print writers than broadcast reporters and include suggested questions (do not be surprised if they do not use them—they are independent-minded). They will read any articles you include.

Interviews for newspapers or magazines may be done in person or on the phone. Be sure that you tape the conversation, and when you set up the appointment ask if the writer will be taping (notes are far less accurate, but acceptable for short interviews that are not too technical). Offer to provide a transcript immediately afterward (if the reporter is on deadline, she will probably tell you she will only have time to rely on her own tape).

Major magazines will want you to fact-check the article before it goes to press—usually that only means quotes and attributed statements will be read to you over the phone to confirm accuracy.

Newspapers will not fact-check, and small to medium magazines will rely on the writer to get things right. In that event, you should tell the writer you would like to look over the first draft before it is turned in to be sure it is factual, appealing to her pride in accuracy. Assure her that you will not suggest changes beyond that. No matter how strongly you feel about the way the story is presented, if your suggestions go beyond important factual corrections, you will be viewed as trying to censor the article.

If you are asked irrelevant hypothetical questions, just respond that you do not speculate on unlikely "what ifs." You can bridge to a discussion of something related, like the firm's future.

If the interview is for a general article about the topic and you only want to be an unattributed source, specify this in advance and be sure you get a clear response from the writer on the tape as to how you are to be identified (a company executive, an industry insider). If your information is very sensitive, do not say anything about it unless you are willing to see it in print with your name attached. No matter how friendly reporters may be, they are not your friends and may be tempted to create a sensation by writing an article identifying you as the source, regardless of the agreement. In that event, report the incident to the editor.

 **Question**

What if the article has errors?
Almost every one does and you do not want to alienate the writer by nitpicking. Write a letter to the editor if the mistake is significant, while thanking the publication for publishing the article. The shorter the letter the better—three paragraphs maximum and expect even that length to be edited. Send it on letterhead with your title indicated.

If you are really unhappy with the article and do not feel a published letter is adequate to correct it, ask the editor for space to write an Op-Ed piece. Or go to a competing publication and explain what the article got wrong. They should be delighted to set the record straight with more information than you were willing to disclose originally (now that the cat is out of the bag).

Usually, errors are due to a combination of the writer's lack of expertise and a tight deadline that precludes fact-checking. Sometimes it is the result of an overeagerness to get a scoop and a tendency to root for the underdog, even when the big dog happens to be right on the issues. But do not let this facet of working with the media make you see them as adversaries. If you clam up, reporters will get the story anyway from some other source, perhaps an unfriendly one.

Online Interviews

In recent years, there has been an increasing interest in two very distinct types of interviews using online capabilities. The first uses instant messaging software on Web sites devoted to a particular subject. The questions may come from a reporter and/or the audience. Chatting this way requires the ability to type short answers quickly, and you should have some prepared for the questions you think you will get. You can refer the audience to further detail on your Web site. If you can exploit this medium, you will probably find yourself way ahead of your competitors.

You can also conduct interviews by e-mail (this is especially acceptable to small publications that otherwise would not deserve time with a business leader, for example). While these could take place live, that is not the best way to use this opportunity. Instead, have the reporter submit questions; you can type up answers at your leisure on a laptop or BlackBerry while waiting for a meeting or when you are flying. This allows you to spend more time thinking about the proper response. You will need to allow further exchanges for clarification and expansion of the answers. E-mailed interviews generally come out more articulate and accurate, since a publicist can help the interviewee with background for answers. To make them seem like a real conversation, make the wording informal.

E *ssential*

Readers of an e-mail interview do not have to know that it was conducted this way—it is irrelevant, but there is still something of a stigma if the reporter does not talk directly with the executive.

Press Conferences

Press conferences are risky unless you have a very strong news hook and the media are eager to grill you to get details that were not in a related press release. If you invite them to come to a press event or to cover a speech and interview afterward, do not expect all of those who make a commitment to be there to actually show up. Very often there are news events that take priority in the editor's mind, the reporter is reassigned at the last minute, and you will not be advised. Hence, go into overdrive to invite every possible member of the press to be there, no matter how obscure. Try also filling the room with other interested parties who may have questions, such as vendors, customers, or community leaders. Provide press kits, a PA system, and refreshments.

 *Question*

What if hardly any reporters show up at my event?
Analyze why and apply the lessons to your next attempt. You can still put up a transcript or audio clip of the speech or press conference and get some mileage out of it. Or the press release will be adequate.

Schedule at a time when the press may be able to attend (10 A.M. weekdays is good, as is Saturday morning, when there is little other news) and set up the event in a convenient location—at the company or a hotel that is centrally located for the media most likely to be there.

Send media alerts as far in advance as you can, then again the day before and follow up with calls to confirm attendance.

For broadcast media, if you have a visual element such as a chart or a product to show, mention that to attract interest.

Crisis Communications

According to Ian Mitroff, author of *Why Some Companies Emerge Stronger and Better from a Crisis*, very few companies have any truly useful plans for dealing with emergencies and the need to inform the media as these unfold. After 9/11, there was a flurry of effort, he notes, but then complacency took over and most organizations are back to their prior bad habits, such as maintaining silos of information in different departments. "The level of denial among very bright people is high, they're not often in touch with their emotions, and they can be victims of their hubris," Mitroff explains.

The number one rule for dealing with a crisis is that you should never wait to build your relationships with the press until you have an emergency. Establish your credibility long in advance and when you face a situation where you do not have all the information the media want immediately, the press will cut you some slack.

 **Alert**

> Never say, "No comment." The media will assume you have the information they want, but it is embarrassing, so you are withholding the details. You then become the enemy and reporters will go to other sources willing to talk, perhaps your competitors or disgruntled employees. Do not speculate; tell journalists what you know and assure them you will keep them informed.

Do not overreact. It is tempting to get defensive or to blame someone else under pressure for a response. Wait until management has some clarity about the nature of the crisis before saying anything other than acknowledging the problem and an investigation of the facts. Follow a crisis management plan that includes fact sheets to give the media general background about the company.

Provide a place for the press to work with lights, electricity, phones, chairs, desks, and Internet connections.

PR guru Harold Burson's advice is that if you have made a mistake, admit it, take responsibility to make things right, and provide all the details as soon as you can. The worst thing, he says, is to let the facts dribble out over a long time.

Remember that a plan to manage a crisis that is only a plan on paper means nothing. Do a drill and learn from the results, otherwise you will be practicing during a real crisis.

The bottom line on dealing with the media is that you need to put a fair amount of effort into cultivating reporters if you want to be interviewed or have a speech covered—at all. The technical aspects of articulating your message are the last part of that process and you can never be too prepared.

CHAPTER 13

Becoming a Pro: Getting Started

If you have been a passionate debater for years, are leading highly rated workshops at work, or were a hit as the keynoter at the alumni dinner, you may be attracted to the idea of being paid to speak on a larger stage. Whether you want to keep your day job and be hired to address gatherings occasionally or wish to ultimately make a career switch to become a full-time professional speaker, there are a lot of issues to consider if you want to be successful.

Getting Paid to Speak

According to Success Motivation Institute, there are nearly two million meetings a year with opportunities for outside speakers. Many of those who are hired to address these meetings are full-time professional presenters—motivational speakers, consultants, trainers, or experts who left their jobs because they became interested in teaching others about their cutting-edge ideas. Others want to continue as, say, senior executives, professors, authors, dentists, or chefs, because they are high achievers, but also enjoy having the influence and high profile (not to mention the extra income) that occasional public speaking engagements can provide. Many of the steps you need to take to get from freebies to fees are the same, regardless of the path you want to pursue.

Are You Sure You Want to Do This?

Vickie Sullivan, president of Sullivan Speaker Services, *www .sullivanspeaker.com*, says that before you charge off to be in the glamorous limelight of professional speaking, you need to ask yourself some hard questions:

- Do you realize this involves more time selling yourself to potential hirers than doing actual speaking?
- Do you enjoy running a business? If you have not been an entrepreneur before, you may not realize that success requires a lot of skills beyond speaking ability.
- If you are in a relationship or have children, what will be the impact of extensive travel?
- Do you have a personal network that will help you get referrals to speak? (Speakers often get hired by recommendation.)
- Perhaps most importantly, can you invest $50,000 until your fees put you in the black? That is what she estimates is the typical start-up expense. Do not count on your talent, good looks, and luck to get a fast start on the process.

Vickie says that it is critical that you leverage a speech during the "honeymoon period," right after it is given. A positive reaction fades quickly, she notes: reach out to those from the audience who gave you their cards and give them ideas to take the relationship with you to the next level, such as one-on-one career counseling or corporate consulting.

Picking Topics

Telling prospects who could hire you to speak that you are able to talk "about anything" lets them know that you are not a professional, you just want the limelight. It is like an actor who admits that his real interest is in becoming famous, not perfecting his craft. The best speakers are passionate about their subjects and want to get audiences excited about them, too. They are on a mission. Trying to get paid public engagements comes with risk—of a speech not going over well, of attracting a small audience, of no one even being willing to pay you. You will also be investing time (to write, practice, market, travel) and energy to be successful, so you had better be totally committed to the importance of what you want to talk about. That will enable you to be persistent in the face of rejection, something that comes with the territory for any start-up project. You probably already have some favorite subjects—but they need to be topics that people will invest their own money and time to listen to (or their company will pay for and give them time off to attend). Of course, you also have to sell prospects on you as an expert and someone who can change the lives of listeners. The first choice to make is whether you want to target the general public or business.

The Personal Market

Love, health, and money are always hot topics—in theory. There is going to be a lot of competition for the attention and dollars of the public for lectures with general titles like "Finding Your Soul Mate," "Lowering Your Risk of Heart Disease," and "Investing in Stocks." Other speakers may have years of professional speaking experience, they may be recognized as authorities because they have written books on their subject, and may be investing money in marketing to those who hire speakers.

To start getting paid engagements, you need to find a distinctive angle, a niche that has not been overworked, preferably something you can claim expertise in (even if there is a little "smoke and mirrors" involved in the sales pitch). Perhaps, taking the above examples, you could talk about "Using Astrology to Find Your Soul Mate," "Three Little-Known Strategies for Preventing Heart Disease," or "The Next Hot Technology for Investors." You can get ideas by researching and brainstorming. Browse the Amazon and BN.com book lists for your general topic, read reviewer comments, and jot down aspects that you might be able to explore in depth. Then google each phrase that defines a niche and add "speaker" and see what comes up. Also, check your specific topic against the mastering listing service *www .seminarinformation.com* (which is a good outlet for publicity, once your settle on your topic). And look for articles about the subject you are considering in mass circulation magazines, at the newsstand, and in online and offline archives.

Alert

Do not forget that you know a lot more about the subject than your audience. Be careful not to say anything important that assumes knowledge listeners may not have, and do not use undefined jargon.

If you do not see your proposed specialty discussed much in recent books or articles, that could mean one of two things. It may just be something there is not enough interest in—at least not to pay for a presentation. Or you could just be ahead of your time (imagine even five years ago the number of people who would have attended a seminar on Wi-Fi or eating organically); you may have uncovered a subject that has not yet been exploited—the next big thing. If it is the latter, you still have some serious selling to do, to convince people to attend (and if you are successful, you can expect a lot of competition soon).

In any event, you do not simply want one topic. You should have a constellation of related subjects you can talk about in different formats.

Your income and marketing plan may call for giving a free introductory ninety-minute lecture with enough substance that it whets the appetite of attendees to pay for a weekend course. Real estate investing seminars often utilize this two-part approach. Or, if you are traveling to another city to speak to a convention of coin collectors, you could offer to teach breakout sessions about detecting counterfeits and ancient Roman coins.

Business

Marketing to companies and business convention organizers is an easier task because there are budgets to be spent on speakers for slots that must be filled. Sometimes consumer-oriented topics are of interest here, too—how to find a balance between work and personal life or staying healthy when traveling a lot for business.

But mostly, firms are going to pay for classes because they recognize the need for constant improvement to compete. It is always a challenge to translate customer service from a slogan on the wall and make it real in the training of employees. By definition, the average sales person could learn from the masters of the game. And everyone can benefit from learning about how technology is going to change work in the next few years.

You can break down your general topic to provide more in-depth treatment in longer workshops after your main speech. If you spoke about technology trends, you could show how these will impact the way suppliers and customers will interact with the attendees' firms, you could review specific products in emerging categories, or provide hands-on training for emerging products.

E ssential

Professional speaker Alan Weiss says that if you are asked to reduce your fee to get a speaking engagement, ask what value the buyer wants to eliminate. "Buyers may love to reduce fees, but they hate to reduce value." Offer different packages with different values based on the objectives, measures of success, and desired outcomes of the meeting.

Alan Weiss, in *Money Talks: How to Make a Million a Year as a Speaker*, advises translating the typical speaker's title for a topic into language aimed at the buyer objectives. So "conduct sales training" becomes "improve sales closing rates"; talking about employee stress reduction is turned into "improve productivity"; "instill customer service attitude" is really about improving customer retention rates. He says that speakers should address "process" issues, rather than "content," so that their specialties can be applied to many industries. "Improving teamwork" and "better decision making" have many potential customers in different types of businesses.

Testing Topics

There are a number of other considerations in choosing a subject, beyond the fact that you have something to teach to others that could be of benefit and the extent of competition. Among these are the health of the general economy (nationally or in the regions where you want to speak), whether the industries you are targeting are growing and competitive (motivating them to invest in learning how to stay ahead), and how much you are able to invest in marketing a particular topic to a target audience (given whether it is likely to attract sustained interest).

E ssential

Subscribe to trade magazines and go to industry conventions for your specialty to pick up ideas for emerging hot topics. There is so much news that even though many people know about something new, very few will have integrated the information into their workplace practices. That is an opportunity for you to entice them to learn more.

The easiest way to test the viability of your proposal, assuming you have sufficient credentials, is to get yourself invited to a regional trade or general business conference as an unpaid speaker. There is no stigma to being unpaid; company representatives and industry consultants often speak or serve on panels just for the exposure, and organizers will be happy to consider you if you seem to be offering value.

Or you can put on a test workshop and invite employees of medium-size local companies (they have education budgets and are less bureaucratic than big corporations). Ask for the person who makes decisions about hiring trainers for your field of expertise and see if she will either pay an irresistibly low figure for workers to attend or at least give your seminar internal publicity and leave it up to individuals whether to participate. Supplement this with mailers to business owners or the appropriate person at small firms. Ads in a local business journal may be helpful. If response is weak, it means you need to rethink the total offering.

Setting Up a Speaking Business

Once you have a set of topics you have road tested and know will be in demand, the next step is presenting yourself as a professional speaker, which starts with a basic office and Web site.

Most new speakers will want to keep expenses under control by initially working from home. For under $20 a month, you can install a second phone line with voicemail that allows messages to be picked up remotely. List this as the office number, along with your cell phone, on business cards and stationery (if you do not want calls at all hours, indicate your business hours and time zone). The primary home line can be used for outbound calls, whether for business or personal, and can also be hooked up to a fax machine (receiving automatically when you are out). As you become more successful, you can add a separate line for personal calls.

Every professional speaker needs a Web site. Include your photo, contact information (including street address for packages), fax number, and e-mail (which should be checked every few hours). A basic site these days can be set up for free using software provided by your Internet Service Provider, or a professional can do it for under $1,000. If you want to sell merchandise and have credit card security, then you will need to add $500–$1,000 to the cost. You also need to be ready to fulfill orders frequently.

Alert

A common mistake in business is to turn over Web site design to a technology whiz who then puts in all the bells and whistles. You end up with a slow-loading Web site with a lot of distracting front elements or a requirement to install Flash video software to even enter the site. Instead keep it simple and visitor-friendly.

You will also need a presentation folder to hold a speaker kit, which should include:

- A one-page biographical sketch that stresses your relevant career experience. This is not a resume, but a sales pitch on why you are the expert the public should listen to about your topic. Mention awards you have received, related articles or books you have written, and the most important venues where you have spoken. Or, if you are an expert, but are thin on evidence to support that claim, make a general statement that you are recognized as an expert in your field (by at least your former boss or customers).
- A photo of you.
- A few paragraphs about each of your subjects on separate pages (these are called one-sheets). Stress benefits to be gained by attendees.
- If possible, an audiotape or CD of one of your presentations.
- One or a few articles you have written on the topics you are promoting.
- Articles others have written about you (nothing fluffy, such as photos of you at social events). If you have books, include a few reviews.

- If you can get a testimonial praising the value of a speech someone heard, even if it was not paid for, include that, either on stationery from the organization or put a few recommendations together on a single page of short quotes.
- A list of your services and fees (you can include short versions of your presentations for smaller groups at lower rates, as well as intensive weekend workshops).

A cover letter introducing yourself and referencing any conversation you had should go with the kit to prospective sponsors.

As you put money in the bank and raise your fees, you can upgrade the kit to include more impressive endorsements, a slick brochure, fancier folder, action shots of you speaking, a video, and so forth.

Contracts and Invoices

Even if you find yourself mostly signing the hirer's contract, you should have your own contract, approved by a business attorney, to remind you of the issues you need covered in any agreement. A 25 to 50 percent nonrefundable deposit is standard in the speaking industry, with the rest paid at the event, but be prepared that some will not pay the balance for thirty days after the presentation (you can offer a discount for early payment).

E ssential

Many new speakers are unaware that companies and associations often have a separate education budget that can pay for workbooks or other materials you can provide to the audience at a profit.

Fees for a one-hour speaking engagement typically run $1,000 to $7,000 for an hour. You can try to get more by offering workshops, perhaps repeated several times during a conference or on different subjects. The longer you talk, the more you should get.

You may want to consider a lower fee if the audience is expected to have potential buyers for company workshops, consulting opportunities, or products you sell. Or you may discount the first presentation as a loss-leader to entice attendees to a more expensive seminar at the conference or to sign up for personal coaching sessions.

If you are going out of town, you also need to specify in the contract whether your travel expenses (flight, transportation to and from airports, parking) are paid for separately or are considered covered by the lump sum for the speech. Usually, a hotel room will be provided, but be very clear about this and any food arrangements.

Alert

Professional speaking guru Lilly Walters advises having one set fee for your standard talk, regardless of whether you are addressing a local group or going out of town. The tendency, she says, is for buyers to think that if you are willing to discount to locals, that is your real price even when you have to travel. Word also gets around and those who paid higher get upset.

Another way to make up for a low-paying gig is that you can ask if it is okay if you sell products at the back of the room after your speech. These can be your own books and related ones by others, special reports, tapes of prior speeches, products, and courses that are Web-based, on video or audio tapes, or conducted by mail or teleconference. Only half of professional speaker revenue comes from being at the podium.

One of the most sensitive issues is that the sponsor often expects to make money selling tapes of your speech as part of the package deal for hiring you. In the beginning, as you are establishing demand for your talks, this may be okay, but you can ask to have the standard contract altered. The preferred wording could forbid them to tape you, designate that the tapes are only to be sold at the event (not to be sold by the organization later, as is often the case), or you might propose profit sharing or a flat fee to you per tape.

If your speech is not being taped (video or audio), make arrangements to have it done professionally, then you can start selling tapes or using them in your speaker kit. Or you can make an adequate audiotape with a high-quality digital recorder on your belt attached to a lapel microphone. Obviously, you only want to sell tapes of your best presentations, so review the tape before listing this as an available product.

Marketing Locally

There are several ways to start getting paid to speak. Typically, you should begin by pitching to local companies, organizations that hold regional conferences, or via continuing education courses in your area, like those held by Learning Annex, colleges, or professional associations. This relieves you of the risks of investing time and money in trying to attract attendees to your own seminars right off the bat and gives you the experience you need to move up to being booked into national venues by speakers' bureaus.

E ssential

Be sure to put a copyright notice on your handouts, to remind everyone that this is not material that they should expect to be allowed to photocopy and mass-distribute to their associates, customers, and friends.

You can also become involved in multiple chambers of commerce to network for leads. Or join a chapter of Toastmasters, which can provide not only help in perfecting your presentation, but connections that may lead to paid speaking engagements.

If you have a topic of interest to a particular industry, you may want to start out by talking at a luncheon for no fee, while giving attendees a handout with information about in-depth training or your consulting services. You can then expand this two-step process to industries with similar business issues and to their suppliers.

You may be able to convince a company to sponsor a seminar that will appeal to its customers. For example, a do-it-yourself store may believe your speech about color compatibility and home design will stimulate sales and will certainly be appreciated by customers as a free service from the store.

E ssential

During questions and answers, pass around a form to get feedback about your speech. Did you cover everything they wanted addressed? How would they rate your presentation in terms of new information? From the standpoint of applying your recommendations? Would they be interested in knowing more about the subject?

Offer to customize material for a group for an additional amount. Study the organization's documents and Web site and interview leaders to understand its history, special interests, and problems, which can be incorporated into your standard presentation, workbook, and handout. You can also collect anecdotes of experiences that provide cases to illustrate your themes. It should take surprisingly little time to tweak the basic presentation and make it much more valuable to a specific audience.

Find out from the nearest convention center and key hotels what organizations are booking meetings there, as far in advance as possible. Then approach those groups and offer to speak, especially if you can give the topic a local twist (an overview of the local industry and business opportunities; a review of unusual museums they may want to visit while in town; the history of the women's movement in your state).

Offer an incentive at every speech for people to give you their business cards or to sign up on your mailing list that is being passed around. Be sure to include a space for e-mail address. You might offer a drawing for a free night at a local hotel or an article about the ten most important tips for a related topic you did not cover in detail (at a basic real estate seminar, you might offer further information on buying foreclosures).

CHAPTER 14

Becoming a Pro: The Big Time

The best-known speakers have usually put in many years of public speaking before being acclaimed as the hot new thing (not to mention spending years as practitioners in their specialties). Expect to work very hard and be patient a long time before you achieve celebrity status. If you have selected the right topics, honed your presentation based on audience feedback, worked the local paid circuit, and cultivated a referral network, you are ready to move up to the national—even international—stage.

Marketing to Major Buyers

The next step, after being thoroughly established as a regional speaker, is to make your pitch to those who either hire speakers for major events or who are the gatekeepers to the decision makers. If you have not already done it, it is time to join one of the organizations for professional speakers. The key ones are:

- National Speakers Association:
  www.nsa.org
- Canadian Association of Professional Speakers:
  www.canadianspeakers.org
- American Society of Training and Development:
  www.astd.org
- International Federation for Professional Speakers:
  www.iffps.org

These hold regional chapter showcases where you can let others hear you, which becomes a way to get leads (and blessed are those who give because they shall receive, so always be proactive and generous in helping fellow speakers).

You should also join one or more organizations for the trades relevant to your topics, read their magazines, and go to their meetings to learn, to network, and, eventually, to speak. Some attendees will be potential buyers for meetings at companies.

 **Alert**

It will hurt your credibility as an expert if you have typographical errors in the material you give to attendees, making them wonder if you are also sloppy with checking your facts. If you are not great at proofreading, get someone who is to help.

Nonbusiness meetings do not have a lot of buyers for paid speeches attending their conventions, of course, but if you give a particularly good presentation, you may be approached by someone who knows of opportunities. Associations for seniors may be interested in seminars on health, hobbyists will pay for workshops with experts, and sports enthusiasts will flock to those who can entertain and inspire them.

Business Associations and Hiring Resources

Many regional and national organizations bring together buyers for speaking engagements at regional and national showcases:

- Hospitality and Sales Marketing Association
- American Society of Association Executives
- Society of Human Resource Management

- Insurance Conference Planners Association
- Meeting Professionals International
- The International Association of Speakers Bureaus
- The National Association of Campus Activities

At nonshowcase meetings, have an exhibit table to make contacts. You can also place ads in newsletters and use direct mail to members.

E ssential

Be aware that meeting planners at companies usually do not make the final decision about whether to hire a speaker. The planner's boss may be the one that does this or it could be someone else. But you want to market to the planners because getting them enthusiastic about you may influence the decision.

Douglas Publications, at *www.salesmansguide.com*, publishes four printed and CD-Rom directories about organizations and companies that hire speakers: *Corporate Meeting Planners*; *Medical Meeting & Event Planners*; *Association Meeting & Event Planners*; *Religious Meeting & Event Planners*.

There are 7,500 organizations listed in a reference book that can be found at many libraries: *The National Trade and Professional Associations of the United States*.

The largest online speaker-matching service is *www.speaker match.com*, which has over 1,000 speakers and 3,000 organization members who hire them.

Speakers' Bureaus

Lilly Walters heads up *www.motivational-keynote-speakers.com*, which has put together a list of 800 speakers' bureaus. This is a reliable source of firms whose primary work is to find their speakers some paying engagements, unlike many commercially available "speakers' bureau" mailing lists, which are filled with individual speakers who will sometimes pass on leads.

Walters says that not until you are earning at least $2,000 per speech should you consider joining a bureau. She lumps together in this category other types of go-betweens, including agents, personal managers, meeting production companies, meeting planners, and brokers who negotiate between buyers and speakers they do not represent exclusively, since much of the advice applies to all of these. Speakers' bureaus typically charge 25 percent of the speaking fee (they may also have a membership charge and require advertising in their catalogs).

Alert

Do not pay a large membership fee to join a speakers' bureau that "promises" to get you paying gigs. Until they try marketing you, a bureau has no idea whether it can match you up successfully with buyers.

When you are registered with more than one bureau, you may find several claiming to have set up a particular engagement for you because all of them were called by the buyer and they all gave you a recommendation. Walters generally recommends awarding the commission to the first bureau that calls to ask if you will accept a speaking date, even if that is not the one that is eventually awarded the contract. Bureaus are really working to please the buyer, their customer, so in the long run it pays for them to set up all the contracts they are asked to do by the buyer, even if they are not getting a commission from you.

If a buyer comes directly to you, it is vital to find out if she heard about you from a bureau so that you can turn over the contract to that bureau. If the buyer cannot remember, make a note to that effect and, if you want to get a bureau to love you, send the buyer to your favorite one to handle the contract details.

A bureau can arrange for you to appear at association speaker showcases and may offer a lot of helpful services beyond getting you hired, including presentation critiques, videotape/CD production, and secretarial services when you are on the road (such as sending out packets on request, answering e-mail, and forwarding calls).

E ssential

If you are new to being paid as a speaker, you may want to affiliate with a young bureau, which will be as hungry as you and have fewer clients to promote. Of course, there will be a trade-off in experience and contacts.

Walters mentions lots of ways to endear yourself to speakers' bureaus, the primary ones being:

- Put the bureau's contact information on everything you hand out, indicating they book your speaking engagements.
- You are able to clearly explain in one sentence why your presentation is different from other speakers on the topic.
- You only call the bureau every few months, preferably outside prime calling hours, and keep the call to the point (also keep e-mails to a minimum).
- You return bureau calls within minutes, not days.
- You are pleasant to work with and their customers do not complain about your behavior.
- You have accurate expense reports that are consistent with the contracts.
- You call after an event is set up to report how it went.

You may be able to find a personal management agency that will help promote you, as well, rather than having to rely entirely on bureaus, which serve the buyers' needs. A manager will need to be paid anywhere from a few hundred to a few thousand dollars a month as a retainer, plus marketing expenses, and they also take a small percentage of the speaking fee.

 **Alert**

Many speakers belong to lead-sharing groups, and helping other speakers is a good way to build up referrals from them. However, do not share leads generated from an event set up by a speakers' bureau. Those leads go to the bureau.

Test-Marketing Your Own Seminars

The most labor-intensive way to get paid to speak is to set up your own workshops, independent of organizational sponsorship. But if you want more income, have exhausted the immediate opportunities to speak at other forums, and are not yet ready to join a speakers' bureau, this can be a very profitable way to go. Because a lot of your own time and money is going to be at risk, however, you want to be sure you have a topic and battle plan that is going to work.

Choose a location that is tasteful and easy to get to for your target audience, schedule it when prospects are likely to be able to go (a two-hour business luncheon downtown, cocktails after hours, a full weekend workshop), and price it based on similar courses. You can then try different means of promoting a test seminar, the most common being newspaper ads and direct mail, because these are low-cost relative to radio and TV. Magazines will generally have rates too high for an initial test.

For a business audience, try placing an ad in a local business publication, which will have less expensive rates than the main daily newspaper. A specialized publication that goes to the members of the industry you believe will be most receptive would be even better and less expensive because of its small circulation. You could also place an ad in the regional edition of a national publication, such as the *Wall Street Journal*.

 Fact

Color ad prices are much higher than black-and-white and newspapers often have limited color capabilities. You can test a four-color (full color) ad in a magazine, but are likely to be disappointed with the results relative to money spent. You can attract attention and make an emotional connection with the reader without color.

For a consumer program, find a publication whose readers are likely to have a similar demographic profile to one you will be using for the posttest program.

Generally, a quarter-page black-and-white ad (white print on a black background will catch even more attention) is the best bet because it is large enough to catch as much attention as a half-page ad at a fraction of the price. Ask for the upper part of a right hand page, even if you have to pay more for preferred positioning. The business section is the obvious place for business seminars, but unless your topic fits a particular section (such as cars or real estate), the first section of a paper is going to be seen by more readers. Sunday is the best day to run, because more people spend more time with the paper. Naturally, it also costs more than ads during the week.

Use an appropriate mailing list (more on this later) to send a brochure to a small number of people, relative to what you plan for the main marketing push. Ask respondents who call how they heard about the seminar (put a seminar code by the phone number and by the Web site address for those who register that way). You can then change the different elements based on the reaction and based on which medium produced the most cost-effective response. Testing will allow you to pick the right subject, title, and price—or let you know that your plan is way off base and save you from financial disaster.

E ssential

Getting a 1 percent response to direct mail is considered successful, but not all of those will actually sign up for a seminar. It is, therefore, critical to first test what type of letter gets the best response before doing a mass mailing. You will probably have to test several times to know how to maximize concrete results.

Seminar marketing guru Howard Shenson, in his classic 1990 guide *How to Develop and Promote Successful Seminars and Workshops*, says that workshop providers that continuously test different elements to see which changes produce better results are much more profitable. The testable items can include dozens of things, such as:

- Time and place
- Color and quality of paper
- Length of letter
- Discount for full payment with registration or installment payments
- Limited time offers
- Inviting readers to call a recorded message or go to a Web site for more information
- Timing the mailing to be received when ads are running
- Photographs, illustrations, or no art
- Use of underlines, italics, and bold

- One, two, or four colors
- Offering a gift
- Doing a follow-up mailing to the same list

Shenson says that whether to place the marketing emphasis on ads or direct mail depends on a variety of factors, but, as a rule, direct mail is more cost-effective for an identifiable and specialized group for which there is a list (e.g., local subscribers to a bird-watching magazine for your workshop on identifying rarely seen birds in your region). These will often pay a higher price for a course.

 Fact

Hiring a publicist or doing basic public relations work yourself (see Chapter 11) is a good way to augment advertising and direct mail. One survey showed that publicity is the third most cost-effective method of promoting seminars, just behind direct mail and ads in newspapers and ahead of ads in business magazines.

Advertising is more likely to work best when you want to reach a broader audience that is also likely to read a particular publication (you are teaching a course on cost-effective home repairs and want to reach homeowners who are readers of the daily newspaper). In that event, the seminar should probably be more moderately priced than one that can be promoted primarily by direct mail.

Cable television can be cost-effective for promoting seminars, but the reason the rates are low compared with broadcast stations is that there are rarely measurements of the size of the audience being regularly reached. Another negative of cable advertising is that you generally have to buy a package that includes channels whose viewers are not in your target audience. If it does seem attractive anyway, beware buying the cheapest time slots, since they are discounted for good reason (the same can be said of radio).

Putting Together an Effective Mailer

The recipient of a direct mail brochure will spend about three seconds deciding whether to read it or toss it out. If she does read it, she may quickly decide the seminar is not something she wants to attend. If she does want to go, getting her to respond and pay is another step. To get an adequate profit, the rule of thumb is you need at least a 2:1 ratio of total receipts to promotion cost per 1,000 brochures mailed. To get there, consider the following ways to improve the response.

Getting Attention

An envelope without any message on the outside and cryptic sender identification will often provoke recipient interest enough to open it. If it is larger than a #10 envelope, that can make it stand out in the mail. Unlike ads, adding at least one color and a quality photo to the letter can improve response.

 Fact

There are no hard rules about color use because it depends on the colors of brochures the recipient has been getting recently. Boredom soon sets in and what prompted attention initially no longer will work. Just make a brochure or letter attractive and do not worry too much about the precise colors used.

The higher the cost of the workshop, the more copy you should expect to need. Other seminar providers have found that not only is longer copy required to convince people to part with their money, but also by following this practice, they have conditioned prospects to expect long letters.

The key benefits of attendance must be stressed in the headline and in bold throughout. Describe yourself primarily in relation to the topic. It may be commendable that you have a degree from Harvard in English, but that will not get people to come and listen to you talk about investing. Hands-on experience in the field is clearly preferable to simply being an academic expert. Business professors do not necessarily really know how to run a company. Other tips include:

- If you are providing a workbook or other tangible item, describe it.
- Use conversational English and avoid overly intellectual phrases, jargon, and clichés.
- Make it easy to sign up and pay (set up a merchant account with a bank so you can take credit cards and also enable registration via your Web site). Provide an incentive to pay early, such as a gift at the door (like a copy of your book).
- Provide a generous cancellation policy, such as until two days before the event. This makes people feel secure about committing (even with this, only 2.5 percent cancel on average).

Using Mailing Lists

The most important aspect of using direct mail is list selection. Standard Rate and Data's *Direct Mail List Source* provides detailed information on the 55,000 primary commercially available mailing lists and is available online by subscription for $649 on *www.srds.com*. It might also be found at any library with a good business reference section. There are probably three times as many other lists available through list brokers (under Mail Lists in the Yellow Pages) or directly from original sources (small associations or publications may not have done much to market their lists). If you can get a list of seminar attendees or subscribers to a publication that fits your topic precisely, you will be going a long way toward success, but put a lot of thought into who is likely to attend and research the lists accordingly.

Generally speaking, the higher the cost of the list, the more valuable it is—for the demographics of those on the list and how frequently it has been updated. Most lists will come with a guarantee about the percentage of bad addresses. You can also ask for references to other customers who have used a particular list to get feedback.

The best strategy is to test out several lists with the same letter to see if there are notable differences. For small tests, you can put together the mailing yourself. A commercial mailing house is essential and very affordable if you are going to do a large one, and you may want to use bulk mail to save on postage, unless you are marketing a high-cost seminar. Keep in mind, though, that it can take a week or two or even more for a local bulk mailing to arrive. Plan to have the piece arrive between four and seven weeks before the event, a range that is neither so early that recipients will put off registering, nor so late they have made other plans.

E ssential

A list broker or a mailing house can merge and purge duplicates in multiple lists if you are renting several that may have significant overlaps. But check the price of doing this against the guarantee of bad addresses to be sure this is cost-effective.

Remember to code your brochures or letters for different lists so that you will match up the responses to determine results.

Selecting Out-of-Town Facilities

By the time you are ready to conduct workshops in other cities, you will know quite a bit about hotel meeting rooms and independent conference facilities.

The critical issues will include:

- Easy access for your target audience at the time scheduled.
- A safe area and one that is convenient to entertainment at night if you are holding a multiday program.

- Moderate pricing—you do not need to hold meetings at the most expensive hotels unless that is what your prospective audience definitely will expect because of your theme (e.g., "How Millionaires Invest").
- Friendly and helpful staff.
- Efficient food service or convenient restaurants. Pay close attention to deadlines for reserving the number of people for meals that are included in the seminar fee, as well as the deadline to change meeting rooms if your attendance varies from expectations one way or the other.
- Audio-visual equipment in good condition.
- If you expect to draw attendees from out of town for a multi-day seminar, you should get a conference price to offer them if they stay at the hotel.

Check the rating of the hotel by the Automobile Club of America (AAA), a good indicator for better hotels. Also check hotel and seminar Web sites to find out which are the most popular meeting places and talk with some of the organizations that use them.

Hotel prices are never firm, but will rise or fall depending on estimated demand and how much they think they can get away with charging you. Check competitors and cite their offers to the place where you would prefer to meet. Make them believe you will be coming back to town for more meetings and that the type of people you attract will provide them with valuable word of mouth.

Filling Seats

If it turns out that, despite your best efforts with testing ads and brochures, you have too many seats empty shortly before the event, you could cancel and try to figure out what went wrong. A creative excuse for "postponement" of the seminar would be better than only having a handful of people sitting in a large conference hall.

On the other hand, you might be able to boost the attendance in several ways:

- If your first mailer goes out early and does not bring in adequate response, decrease the price significantly and/or offer something extra (longer event, follow-up miniseminar to drill deeper into a subtopic, another book, a special report, five minutes of one-on-one counseling, etc.). Send first-class to a new list and include as many people as you can afford. Better that you lose a modest amount of money than cancel (remember that you can also count product sales into the revenue and that the attendee list should be worth a lot for follow-up seminars and sales).
- Approach potential sponsors about sending their employees or members at a nominal price (or even free, in return for being able to meet with decision makers for paid training). Or get permission to distribute brochures at companies or groups you did not already cover. If neither of those tactics proves adequate, consider a third-tier organization to which you can extend a free invitation.
- Write an article on the subject for a newsletter that will arrive before your event, for a relevant Web site, or for the local daily or weekly newspaper or a business journal.
- Hire a telemarketer who knows how to talk to your audience. You should consider hiring a freelance marketer to both find speaking engagements and fill seats (until then, plan to spend one full day a week doing the marketing calls yourself).

Whatever happens, remember to be pleasant to everyone you meet, all the time. If word gets around that you are difficult to work with—in the view of the hotel or a sponsoring organization—or that you seemed aloof or preoccupied when attendees wanted to talk with you off the podium, your reputation will take a hit and make people reluctant to work with you or attend in the future. Being a professional speaker is a lifestyle, not just a job.

Sample Persuasion Speech

Time Flies Whether You Want It to or Not
by Jeff Davidson

Jeff Davidson, MBA, the author of The Complete Guide to Public Speaking, *is a work/life balance expert* (www.BreathingSpace.com). *This is a great example of a persuasion speech—it would be hard to disagree with him by the time he is finished. This 2,879-word talk takes at least thirty-five minutes to present, he says. That is a rather slow pace because this is filled with information that needs to be digested slowly and each argument builds carefully on the last one. The speech is particularly notable because of its use of many questions and startling statistics. But Davidson also relies on lists, tips, and quotations to reinforce his points.*

Have you ever considered how much time you have in your whole life, and how much time you've spent on various activities? Suppose you graduated from college at the age of 22, and in the course of your life expect to work about 48 years, bringing you to age 70. Over those 48 years, how much time would you guess you've spent on routine activities such as working, sleeping, watching television, recreating, eating, and commuting?

Here's the typical breakdown, based on various demographic studies and my own calculations:

Working . . . . 16 years

Sleeping . . . . 15 years

Viewing TV . . . . 5–7 years

Recreation . . . . 2–4 years

Eating . . . . 3 years

Commuting . . . . 2 years

Based on researcher's findings, the average American will spend 3,571 hours in the course of a year watching television, listening to the radio, reading newspapers, or being online. Since there are only 365 days in the typical year, that means the above activities consume a little less than 10 hours per day!

It's amazing when you look at the cumulative total of the time you'll spend engaged in these activities during your productive work life. Suppose that you're already 30-something and on average will live another 45 years. Thus, you have about 30 waking years left, and about 20 years to accomplish whatever you're seeking to accomplish. That realization alone may help you focus your time.

If you don't expect to reach age 80, think again. The Society of Actuaries estimates that if you're female and you're 40 years old, your life expectancy exceeds age 85, for males age 80.

On average, most people are likely to live longer than they think they will. The realization that you may live much longer than you think necessitates developing some longer-term perspectives about how you want to spend your life.

When Limits Help

With decades to go, it's easy to get caught in the trap of delaying the activities and events you promised yourself you'd undertake. Whether life seems short and merry or long and boring, there's only so much of it. Architect Frank Lloyd Wright once observed that people build "most nobly when limitations are at their greatest." You can use the limits on your time or resources to achieve your most desired accomplishments.

Consider how productive you are, for example, before you leave for a vacation, or consider how well you do on a task when a deadline has been imposed (even though you might not enjoy having the deadline or like the person who imposed it). As the author of many books, I can testify about deadlines. Each contract imposed deadlines, and these limits actually helped me be productive.

These limits may not always appear helpful or supportive, yet you undoubtedly have many of them confronting you. Here are some examples of limits you may be facing right now:

- You have to pick your kids up by 5:30 P.M. each weekday.
- You have to turn in a work log on Fridays.
- You can work about nine hours daily before your mind turns to mush.
- Your hard drive is almost full, and you won't spring for a larger drive.
- Your contract is ending in 11 weeks.
- You have only 24 minutes left on your lunch break.
- The oil in your car needs changing after another 3,000 miles.
- A loved one is nearing the end of his or her life.
- You get paid every two weeks.

What limits do you face in your career or personal life that you could employ to propel yourself to higher productivity? When you learn to harness these for the benefit they provide, you begin to reclaim your time. I suggest that your daily, primary limit be finishing your day so that you leave work at the normal closing hour.

The Time-Theft Culprit

After examining the problem for many years, sifting through extensive research, interviewing dozens of people, collecting articles, and tapping the minds of many learned people, I found that the No. 1 element that robs people of their time can be boiled down to a single word: Television.

Is it just my perception, or are people now watching TV at all hours? The plug-in drug has got our culture by the throat. In addition to becoming intellectually numb, are people also becoming deaf? (Preliminary data suggests that rising noise levels on society are resulting in increased hearing loss.) People are flipping on the television the first moment that they wake up. They get dressed to it. They drink coffee to it. They eat breakfast to it. They shave or put on makeup all while watching television. Then they trot off to work only to return and, before doing nearly anything else, flip their television back on. Unfortunately, this has become the norm.

The average American watches more than four hours of TV each day, equal to two months of non-stop TV-watching per year, and equal to more than 12 solid years of non-stop TV-watching in the life of a person who lives to age 72.

- 66 percent of Americans watch TV while eating dinner.
- 49 percent of Americans say they watch too much television.
- 19 percent of Americans say they'd like to read or visit friends but have no time!

More than 90 million adults watch television at least two hours on any Monday and Tuesday night—that's at least 360 million viewer-hours. These viewer-hours, if applied elsewhere, could transform the nation. Ah, but you can choose to watch TV whenever you want, can't you? Or can you? Television is a drug, with many of the same side effects as other drugs. And as the Internet becomes an even more dominating aspect of more people's lives, it will compete, or merge, with TV to claim your time.

Oblivion Starts Here

In his book *Amusing Ourselves to Death*, the late Dr. Neil Postman says that entertainment is the dominant force in public discourse in society, affecting the arts, sciences, politics, religion, and education. Certainly entertainment has a necessary function in your life: It stimulates thinking. It can be liberating to your soul. It can give you a break from the monotony of daily living. Of note, entertainment can free you to explore new ways of thinking, new ideas, and new possibilities.

The harm in being over-entertained—which everyone faces—is that your daily life seems to pale by comparison to what you view on the screen. What is the true cost of entertainment? Certainly your time, and usually your money. You're willing to trade these because entertainment expressly is not reality. It's designed to be "superior" to reality—it's more titillating and more engaging. In a 1978 lecture at Indiana University, the late Gene Roddenberry, creator of *Star Trek*, boldly stated: "TV does not exist to entertain you. TV exists to sell you things."

Don't make the erroneous assumption that watching brain-drain TV or listening to shock-talkers on the radio has no impact on your time. They vacuum up time you could have used doing something worthwhile. Turn them off.

When compared to what you see on the screen, your own life may seem dull and plastic. Instead, it is real and holds great potential. Ultimately, the quality of your life and your memories will depend on what you actively did, not what you passively ingested. What will you do in the next month to enrich your life—actually enrich it? Who will you meet? What will you risk?

Consider how much time and energy you're willing to spend with your favorite TV personalities. Now contrast that figure with how much time you actually spend with any of your neighbors. Do you even care about their lives? They are, in fact, flesh-and-blood people with real strengths, real weaknesses, and real lives. They could even become your lifelong friends. Do they offer as much pleasure to you, however, as the fantasy heroes on *CSI*, Matt Damon in his latest role, or Elle McPherson simply posing in garments you'll never own? You might have a reason to like your neighbors: Consider all the expensive stuff they're not trying to sell you.

"I Only Tune In to Stay Informed"

I know people who habitually watch the nightly news believing that this will make them informed citizens. The problem is, most of what passes for news on television isn't news. It's merely a constant rehash of the same stories, over and over.

I'm sorry that there's drug infestation in society, that too many teenagers get pregnant, and that there are homeless people roaming many cities. Unless you're going to take action on any of this stuff, however, watching another report about it doesn't count toward your status as an informed citizen. So, the time you spend watching it is largely wasted.

I'm not saying you shouldn't watch any news. Rather, you need to understand the context in which news is presented. News shows are designed to attract viewers so sponsors can sell things, the same as any other show; they heighten the emphasis on some stories and completely ignore others. As long as you understand the limitations of TV news, watch away. Don't turn off your brain when the news comes on. And remember that there are probably many more productive ways you could be spending that time.

New Routines for New Perspectives

As if you're not watching enough television, what are the chances that you're turning on the radio, cluttering up your mind from that source as well? Consider a friend of mine who liked to listen to a West Coast shock-jock in the morning. Year after year, my friend Bill was titillated on his way to work by the shock-talk.

In essence, he settled for an electronic fix that briefly took him out of his own life and into some form of contemptuous humor that got him through the next 10 minutes (or however long) on his way to work. After all the years of listening, my friend is not empowered, energized, or any better able to face his day. Bill isn't alone; this particular shock-jock has become a multimillion-dollar media franchise and has had strong ratings for more than a decade. If you listen closely to the shock-jocks of the world, you can sometimes detect that they are angry people. They vent their anger through a form of broadcast that has (for whatever reason) become a socially tolerated route to riches.

Instead of listening to the radio on his drive to work, Bill could contemplate what he'd like to achieve for that day. If he has meetings, he could consider some of the points he would like to make. He might visualize having a pleasant lunch with a coworker. He might put on some classical music to ease his mind as he makes his way through the otherwise-unforgiving rush-hour traffic.

If he consciously chooses to play the radio, maybe he'll switch to a provocative news magazine-type show where issues are covered with some depth and perspective. Perhaps he'll tune into something that truly stimulates his intellect.

Of course, he has the option of playing CDs or cassettes. He can listen to famous speeches, motivational programs, or entire books on cassette. He can play cassettes of famous old-time radio programs or listen to the Bible on cassette. By applying a modicum of creativity, he can turn his commuting time into something special. He can turn his use of the television into something special.

Bill has many different pockets of time available. He also has many options to determine how he spends them.

So do you.

10 Steps to Kick Electronic Addiction

1. Go a whole weekend without turning on a radio or television, and if you can, even stay off of the Internet.
2. Call your friends (both local and out-of-town) one evening per week instead of watching any television.

3. Return to hobbies such as stamp collecting, playing a musical instrument, gardening, or playing word games one other weeknight instead of watching TV.

4. Allow yourself to selectively watch two hours of programming each Saturday and Sunday for one month.

5. Permit yourself one high-quality video per weekend during another month. The video has to inspire, inform, reflect history, be biographical, or be otherwise socially redeeming. Stop watching shoot-em-ups, chase scenes, and films that titillate but add little to your life.

6. If you walk or jog with a Walkman, undertake these exercises three times in a row without such a device so you can experience another way to jog: taking in what you pass on your trip.

7. Look for others seeking to wean themselves from electronics. Is there a book discussion group? How about a bowling league, outing club, or biking group?

8. Attend sporting events rather than viewing the same type of event on television. Watching a good high school baseball team or women's collegiate tennis match can be as rewarding as watching major-league baseball or Wimbledon, respectively. And you visibly support the athletes by being there.

9. Recognize that the number of DVDs, videos, CDs, computer games, and other electronic items competing for your attention exceeds the time you have in life to pay homage to them.

10. Recognize that rightly or wrongly, you've been programmed since birth to tune in to electronic media for news, information, entertainment, and diversion. It's by no means your only option.

Easy Math for Reclaiming Your Time

While the cumulative impact of being hooked on electronic media is considerable, the cumulative impact of doing what you don't like to do, such as household tasks, is equally insidious.

Consider the scenario where your career lasts 48 years. 48 years? Yes, graduating college at age 22 and working until age 70. Here's a quick way to see that you need to delegate or cast off those things you don't like to do. Any activity in which you engage for only 30 minutes a day in the course of your 48-year productive work life will take one solid year of your life! Any activity in which you engage for only 60 minutes a day will take two solid years of your 48 years. How can this be so?

Think of it as a mini math lesson most of us never had in school: Numbers That Really Mean Something. One half-hour is to 24 hours as one hour is to 48 hours. That's true by the good old commutative principle of arithmetic. Likewise, one hour is to 48 hours as one year is to 48 years.

When you consume one-forty-eighth of your day (only 30 minutes out of 24 hours) the cumulative effect over 48 years is to consume one year of your 48 years. There's no way around it. If you clean your house, on average, for 30 minutes a day, then in the course of 48 years you've spent the equivalent of one solid year, nonstop, cleaning your house.

If you can't stand cleaning your house (or something else you don't like) for an average of 30 minutes a day, stop doing it. Don't let your house get filthy; hire somebody to clean your house, clean it yourself less often, or find some other alternative. Why? Because the time in your life is being drained; the cumulative impact of doing what you don't like to do, as illustrated above, is that your precious years are being consumed. This is time you simply cannot reclaim under any scenario.

"Well," you say, "that's fine to pay somebody to clean the house, but ultimately I'll be paying people for all kinds of things I don't like to do, just so I can have more time." Exactly.

What things do you know you need to stop doing because they are taking up valuable time in your life? Here are some suggestions:

- Cleaning the house.
- Cutting the grass, or any other yard work.

- Reading the newspaper every day. If it makes you late for work or prevents you from handling higher-priority activities, only do it now and then.
- Fixing your car.
- Cooking.
- Reading junk mail because it's addressed to you.
- Reading every godforsaken e-mail message zapped over to you.
- Answering the phone.

If you enjoy some of these activities, by all means keep doing them. Perhaps you can do them a little less; perhaps there's another way to proceed. Your goal is to delegate or eliminate those tasks or activities which you can't stand doing. One author advises, "Don't manage something if you can eliminate it altogether." Not bad advice.

In Closing

- You're probably going to live longer than you think, but it will be to no avail if your days continue to race by full of frustration and the same old stuff.
- To the extent you can reduce your television viewing, you'll experience an abundance of extra time in your life.
- The cumulative impact of doing what you don't like to do is profound. A 30-minute, 20-minute, or even 10-minute savings per day is significant and increases the amount of discretionary time you have in your life.
- If drudgery sticks you up for either your life's time or your money, which would you rather hand over?
- Don't manage what you can eliminate altogether; simplify what you can't eliminate.

Thank you. You have been a wonderful audience!

Sample Internal Marketing Speech

by Susan Drake

Susan Drake, the author of Light Their Fire: Using Internal Market-ing to Ignite Employee Performance and WOW Your Customers, *is a speechwriter and marketing consultant to major corporations (see www.spellbindersinc.com). This talk is one she gives herself and she delivers it quickly: this is 3,557 words, but takes her only twenty min-utes to get through (that is the maximum amount of time she believes most audiences can pay optimum attention). This is more of an infor-mational speech than the one in Appendix A, but Drake also strives to persuade the audience of her point of view: that companies need to start their marketing with selling their goals to their employees and aligning their practices accordingly. She uses liberal doses of humor, repetition, memorable phrases, and anecdotes. This also has attention-getting opinions, examples, interesting statistics, quotations, tips, and interaction with the audience to make an impact.*

A month or so ago I met a guy. It's not what you think. His name is Brad and he's a server at a Mexican restaurant. My husband and I go there because it's close, the food is okay, in spite of the fact that there's always something wrong. It's the margarita blender or the ice cream freezer or, once, it was even the Coke dispenser. You can't have chips without a Coke. Southerners can't even have breakfast without a Coke.

So on my last visit, when Brad told us about the broken equipment du jour, I said, "Brad, we love to come here, but every time we do you don't have something we want. Can you mention that to the manager?"

Boy, I had made Brad's day. He lit up like a Christmas tree. He scooted into the booth next to me.

"You wouldn't believe how they run this place. I'm a marketing major, and I could tell them a thing or two about how they SHOULD run it." (Lean away) I might mention that although Southerners are known for their hospitality and friendliness, that does not extend to inviting our server to join us for lunch.

As we say in the South, "Bless his heart."

WALK

I was at the airport last month headed for San Antonio. At our gate, a little old lady on a walker was waiting to board a plane. She could barely stand up. But when she got to the gate agent, the woman said, "I have NOT called for boarding, and it would be better for ME if you stood back."

Bless her heart.

WALK

I went to a car dealer and explained that I was prepared to buy a car on the spot provided that they didn't put me through their usual sales routine. Within moments they were doing their dance. So I walked out. The salesman chased me outside asking, "What can we do to make a deal?" Guess he hadn't been listening the first time I told him.

Bless his heart.

PAUSE

Maybe you think that these three stories merely show the difference between good and bad employees, and they don't have anything to do with sales or marketing. Or that I'm a lightning rod for horrendous service.

Or you could surmise that training would take care of the problem. That could be part of it, but there's oh so much more to the story. The moral of the story is that none of these employees realized that they were totally responsible for the loss of a sale and for creating a poor image for their company.

Down in my neck of the woods, there is a lush, green, beautiful vine known as kudzu, brought to the U.S. in the 1930s to help control erosion. Kudzu could be the subject of a horror movie, because it devours everything in its path . . . including automobiles.

When I'm driving down the interstate and I see that beautiful, ubiquitous kudzu, I automatically think: sales and marketing. It's true. Because sales and marketing is an intertwined process in which every corporate leaf is linked, from how you hire people to how you relate to customers.

We're all guilty of platitudes like, "A stitch in time saves nine," and "The early bird gets the worm." How many of you have said, "At our company marketing is everybody's job." Sure, that sounds nice, but what's the reality? Is anybody doing anything deliberate to make it true? If marketing and sales is what your entire company is about, then every single team member must understand your brand, believe in your brand, love your brand and protect your brand. In most companies, it just ain't so.

In my experience, the reason it ain't so is that while most companies are investing millions trying to convince consumers that their toothpaste will give them whiter, straighter, cavity-free teeth, they're spending less than one percent of that to make sure employees believe that every single person in the company contributes to making toothpaste that will give the consumers whiter, straighter, cavity-free teeth. And all at a good value to the customer.

They have lots of external marketing and sales. But they don't have internal marketing and sales. So tell me this: If your employees don't know that they're sales people, how do you expect them to sell?

Internal marketing means selling your company to employees just as you do to your customers. We turn traditional marketing techniques inward to create employee engagement and loyalty. First sell to your employees, then sell to your customers.

One of my clients is Hampton Inn hotels. Hampton's culture is driven by their dedication to satisfying every guest, no matter what it takes. They even have an unconditional satisfaction guarantee that every employee is empowered to invoke. They advertise the guarantee, and research shows that customers are influenced to choose Hampton because of the guarantee.

So here's what happens when you have employees who understand, love and support your brand.

A woman had a problem with her hair dryer, so she called the front desk for a replacement. When the maintenance engineer brought the hair dryer up, she opened the door and her cell phone immediately rang. She turned to the man and motioned to him (indicate her talking on the phone and gesturing). She wanted him to blow dry her hair while she talked. And he did.

He understands that his job isn't delivering hair dryers or repairing equipment. His job is to satisfy every guest every time, no matter what. And he knows it because Hampton does an absolutely phenomenal job of communicating it not just to guests, but also to employees. Their internal message to employees is a mirror image of their exterior message to customers. As a result, every employee—and I mean EVERY employee—understands what it means to do whatever it takes to make the guest happy.

Hampton's maintenance engineer is the product of internal marketing. He knows what the company's goal is, and what he does ultimately convinces the guest that Hampton is the best place to stay.

Sometimes a consultant surprises herself with results. And when I learned about this story I said, hey, if I can get a maintenance engineer to blow dry my hair, I am an even more passionate evangelist for internal marketing.

Can I get an amen?

PAUSE

Let's do a little experiment. Could I have two volunteers please? Thank you. (shaking their hands) Hi, I'm Susan. And your name is? Wonderful. Either of you married? Well, let's overlook that for just a moment. (Man), would you please take this ring, and propose to (Woman)?

Why did you (accept or reject) his offer?

Now what was that guy doing? He was SELLING! He told her what the benefits would be if she married him. And as a result of his selling, they got engaged.

When you get engaged with a romantic partner, AND when you get engaged with your employees, you base the relationship on trust and shared values, and you sustain it with enthusiasm and success.

Thanks. I hope you'll live happily ever after!

According to a poll by Gallup, some of your employees are not fully engaged in their jobs. That's right. They either don't know and understand your values, or they're not buying your toothpaste.

Let's see what you think about how big the problem is: How many of you think that 25 percent of your employees are not fully engaged? How many think it's 60 percent? 70 percent? You're all WAY too optimistic.

Studies show that 80 percent of employees are not fully engaged in their jobs. Eighty percent. And what does that mean? Well, there's an excellent chance that the vast majority of your employees are only moderately loyal, they're probably not selling, and, if they're like Brad, they could even be doing your company harm.

Some years ago I was consulting with a financial services company, exploring why employees felt dissatisfied. A recurring theme in focus groups was that the tellers were often embarrassed because customers came into the bank and asked them about new products or special offers they'd never heard of. Yeah, they're cool when you're sitting at headquarters dreaming them up, but they go nowhere fast if you don't let employees know how cool they are, too. Employees cannot sell if they don't know what they're supposed to be selling.

If you're not engaging employees in the vision, the product, the service and the brand, you're missing a chance to recruit a great sales team. And that will absolutely be obvious on the bottom line.

The employees we interviewed were not engaged. In fact, they were angry at management for not communicating with them. (Turn to an audience member and ask, "What do you think an angry employee says to a customer?" "What would an embarrassed, humiliated employee say?")

Exactly. Bless their hearts.

Let's say you slip up once, and the employees didn't get the word about the new campaign. Even without knowledge of the products, a teller can sell. Here's how: "Yes, Mr. Trump, let me get some information about that new program for you," and scrambled to find out the details. A loyal employee would have done everything he could to protect the company's reputation and serve the customer. A loyal employee would have shared the information with his co-workers so they wouldn't be caught off guard. And the customer would never know that there was a small glitch in the system.

The quickest way to lose customers is to short change your employees in the areas of knowledge, training, tools and empowerment.

I've been around for thirty years in business, and I've seen management fads come and go and come back around again. We've empowered teams, optimized resources, grown our people, one-minute managed them, and turned them into raving fans . . . well, raving, anyway. Go on Amazon.com and search for management books, and you'll find 576,026 books in that category. Seven of which are mine.

With that many experts coming up with so many, many theories, why are companies struggling to differentiate themselves, crying about employee defection, and fighting tooth and nail for sales?

I don't mean to go all Zen on you, but perhaps the answers lie within, grasshopper, which is where true sales begins. Fairfax Cone said, "Advertising is what you do when you can't go see somebody." What he was really talking about was relationship marketing. He was talking about building connections with people. And that's what customers today are looking for: a bond with a brand, with the people who make up the brand.

So guess what: Employees are the people who are going to build relationships. They're the ones who go see somebody—customers. They answer the phone, send out a package, help a co-worker and in many, many ways contribute to the well-being of the organization's relationship with customers. This is no different than what Dale Carnegie wrote about in 1937 followed by Zig Ziglar in 1975. Even Barbra Streisand talked about People who need people.

Relationships and connecting with people is the sales and marketing of the twenty-first century just like it was in the nineteenth or twentieth century. But it goes way beyond the traditional employees who are technically "sales" people on your team.

PAUSE

This kudzu-ish marketing and sales is truly a holistic discipline that involves everyone in your company. And it's the only totally effective approach to creating loyal customers. Since I started out in business thirty years ago, I've always believed that companies are best served by combining internal and external marketing approaches, thus selling from the inside out.

There's a passage in *Alice in Wonderland* where Alice says to the Queen, "There is no use trying; one can't believe impossible things." And the Queen replies, "When I was your age, I always did it for half an hour a day. Why sometimes I've believed as many as six impossible things before breakfast."

Take a moment and imagine this impossible thing: Suppose you could turn all of the disengaged 80 percent into engaged employees. What would the result be? Today you're successful with only 20 percent of your employees turned on and performing well. Think what you could do if you could turn even half of the 80 percent into engaged employees?

I'll tell you what could happen. Engaged companies have 38 percent better productivity, are 56 percent more likely to have higher than average customer loyalty and enjoy about 27 percent more profitability. Maybe you're like Alice, and you think that's an impossible thing. I can assure you it's not. I've seen it.

I've seen manufacturing employees break every one of their production records while reducing their lost-time accidents. That was after we spent just about six months working on internal marketing. I've seen a restaurant chain increase employee enrollment in their benefits plan by 30 percent in one enrollment period after one project-oriented internal marketing campaign. I've seen Hampton Inn undertake a brand-wide initiative that involved 4 million operational changes in 1,300 hotels. All that in just nine months supported by internal marketing.

Want to know how we do it? My associate and I define four characteristics to what we call "E" employees. These are people who are engaged, enabled, empowered and ensured.

(show E Employees slide)

E employees are engaged because they care about their companies. They are enabled because they've been given the tools and knowledge they need. They are empowered to make decisions that benefit the organization. Their performance is ensured because they're held accountable for achieving goals, and they're rewarded and recognized for their success. These are people who are ready to receive their 007 license to sell.

When I started my career in Memphis at Holiday Inns, the company was just about 25 years old. Its founder, Kemmons Wilson, was a sure-fire, dyed in the wool entrepreneur. He was colorful, and funny, and he developed a culture of fanatics. Everybody who worked there could tell you how he got started by owning a popcorn machine, and that he used to select sites by flying over the country, looking down and seeing that some area was a good place to build a hotel. And that Holiday Inn was named after a Bing Crosby movie. They loved the company. Their blood ran green.

Around 1988, Holiday Inn moved to Atlanta. The employees who were left in Memphis started having reunions. Every year. For, let's see, what year is it now? 2005. Okay, they've been having a reunion every year for seventeen years! Those people are still engaged, and they're still selling Holiday Inn.

But how do you build an "E" employee? Can you turn someone who's just collecting a paycheck into someone who would dress up as the Holiday Inn flashing neon sign at a Halloween party? Yes, you can. Here's a start.

Let's say you are getting ready to merge two divisions. It's quite a change-management initiative. You can do it one of two ways. You can put everyone in one building and let them figure things out for themselves, a strategy destined to interrupt all of your customer relationships. Or, you could create an internal marketing plan.

Start by defining what you want to achieve. Specify all of your audiences, just like you would in any marketing program. In this case, the audiences might be the call center, line-level employees, the middle management group, the quality control center, and the senior management team. For one of our clients we identified twenty-four distinct audiences. Every one of them is important.

Next, assess your climate to determine existing opinions, the level of engagement, the willingness to change, and so on. With that information you can begin to craft overriding messages for each group, keeping in mind that everyone wants to know how it will benefit them. Tell them what's happening, when, how and most important "why." Explain how the change will contribute to greater customer satisfaction. Link the event to the overriding company goal.

Decide which vehicles will best carry your message to each group. Notice that the selection of the vehicles is step 5 on our chart. Unfortunately, the companies I've seen start with the message and then go straight to the vehicle, without consideration of effectiveness. I wish I had a dollar for every time I've gone in to consult with a company and they've said, "We need a newsletter." Remember, even if you're dealing with an internal audience, you're competing with *People* magazine, *Survivor* and Google. The vehicles have to be varied and many. And they have to tell an interesting story.

At this point we diverge a bit from external marketing. Some marketing efforts make use of a spokesperson like the Jolly Green Giant, Ed McMahon or J-Lo. But ALL internal marketing efforts need a highly visible, energetic champion. Find someone at the top of the organization who can motivate people, and is willing to dedicate the time to your plan. Then, seek out the natural champions that exist at all levels. Tap these people to influence peers and others.

Just like Crest toothpaste has to run commercials every day, magazine ads, promotional offers, and so on, internal marketing has to take place regularly, throughout implementation, providing constant reinforcement, recognition and clarification. Communication is the thread that will weave your goal into every facet of the organization.

Finally, how will you know you've succeeded? There's one very clear gauge of success. Walk around the office and watch people. Sense the climate: Is it energizing, or is it draining? Are people smiling and full of ideas, or are they lackadaisical and complaining?

Aside from using your powers of observation and intuition, you'll want clear metrics to judge your achievements. This doesn't mean simply surveying for employee satisfaction, or doing a quality review of the communications vehicles you've used. Who cares if employees are satisfied? We want to know they're impassioned, fired up, all but obsessed.

Look for both tangible and intangible results that are directly tied to your goal. If you're trying to improve call center effectiveness, then check for agent knowledge and attitudes. If you're attempting to reduce accidents in a plant, you must measure the outcome. And if you're hoping to increase engagement among employees, you could measure people's awareness of the brand, their belief in the brand's promise, and their understanding of how to take action to support it.

Product and service? Customer-centric measurements are essential. And not just whether they were satisfied or not. Dig deeper to find out whether they're loyal and would recommend your product to a friend.

Inside the company, outside the company, it's the same story, spun in different ways according to the audience's needs. What you sell to employees, they'll sell to customers. With their words, and with their actions.

For years we've been hearing annoying ads for a car dealer in Memphis called Gossett. You Gossett! is their slogan. A couple of years ago my husband bought a new Jeep Grand Cherokee from them. Our experience with the salesman was so pleasant and hassle free that I ditched my Lincoln Town Car three days later for another Jeep. We actually became brand advocates in spite of their external marketing!

Remember earlier when I told you that I'd shopped for a car and the salesman wasn't smart enough to listen to me when I said I didn't want the same old sales pitch?

Well guess who he lost the sale to: Yep, you Gossett. Their salesman WAS smart, and he listened, and he met my needs. With no hassle. And, as we say in the south, no who-shot-john. It was the start of a beautiful relationship because the service was absolutely flawless.

You know where that kind of service starts? Well, one evening we went to dinner at Benihana, and we sat next to a nice friendly couple. He was wearing a cap with Jeep on it, and he told me, "I sell cars." What dealership, I asked. He said, "Gossett." I proceeded to rave about the service we'd had there and told him we'd bought two cars from them. He couldn't shut me up.

When the meal was over, he asked the server to give him our check. He turned out to be the owner of Gossett. Now that's marketing! HE knows how to show a customer appreciation, and you can bet that his employees know exactly how to treat customers, whether they work in the used car lot, the finance section, the service department or the showroom. Even without Crest, they have a big smile for customers. They all understand that the company's goal is to build relationships with customers at every possible opportunity, even at Benihana.

And I suspect that it's his employees' engagement that has allowed Mr. Gossett to own Gossett Audi, Gossett Chrysler, Gossett Hyundai, Hyundai South, Jeep, Kia, Kia South, Mazda, Mitsubishi, Gossett Motor Cars, Porsche, Volkswagen and several auto parts and body shops. No wonder the guy could buy us dinner! He could buy the restaurant!

Marketing is simple. Invest as much in your relationship with your employees as you do with your customers. Get your employees engaged. Inspire them not to act like Brad.

Say it with me: Bless his heart.

Sample Speeches for Almost Every Occasion

I n this section, you'll find a variety of sample speeches for different occasions. These speeches are meant to serve as models for how you might clearly and effectively organize and present ideas and information in speeches with specific purposes. You'll find that, as they were written for the sake of demonstration, most of them are somewhat generic and relatively short. When writing your own speeches, you usually will want to make them longer and include more details and specific information related to your own particular aim, audience, occasion, and venue. However, you can certainly use the speeches here to provide you with ideas and examples. Included here you'll find speeches on:

(continued)

(Sample Speeches, continued)

Boosting Morale

The poet Theodore Roethke once said, "In a dark time, the eye begins to see." And in the wake of these recent layoffs, in this dark time of tremendous insecurity and uncertainty, it is imperative that we maintain a clear vision—both of the way things are now and of the way they will be.

It probably comes as a surprise to no one that after our merger with Calco Pharmaceutical and the consequential layoffs, I have called everyone together. I am not going to pull any punches in this discussion. You are my staff, and I want to be frank with you. I want to tell you what I know about the immediate future of this company. I want to empower you with these facts. I want to create an atmosphere of security, understandably no easy task when some of our coworkers have just been downsized. But we now need to move forward to ensure our own jobs. And I believe together we can do this. Today, I'm going to share with you the three-step plan that is going to take this company into its next phase of existence.

Let me first say, though, that no more layoffs are in the immediate future. If you are sitting in this meeting listening to me, you do have job security. Please take that in. This company needs you. All of your jobs are essential. This is a fact.

Now for our three-step plan for a better, more lucrative future: merging, identifying, and modifying. Step One: Merging. Change is never easy. Transition is often uncomfortable. But the outcome can reap tremendous benefits for all. The merging phase of the three-step plan is going to be the hardest. The way we are used to doing our work is going to be questioned. Our operations and methods will be closely scrutinized. It is enough to make the most secure worker feel a little shaky. But, hear me, this is just part of the process.

Nothing about this phase is personal. We are not looking to cut back any more. We are looking to move forward.

You will not be alone during this phase of our plan. This is the most important thing for you to remember. I have an open door. If you need help, please come to me. If you need reassurance and guidance, please come to me. If you just need someone to hear your frustration with this process, please come to me. I am not just paying lip service. During this first phase, my sole job is to be there for you and to make this difficult transition easier for you. Your job during this first phase is to become more aware. Pay attention to what is going on; make observations about what is working and what is superfluous. Think about the positive changes you'd like to see here. Keep notes. The more you notice, the more you can participate in the exciting changes taking place.

Awareness leads us into step two of our plan, identifying. We need now to identify changes we need to make; we also need to identify what already works. Your notes and observations from phase one are critical in phase two. If you're happy here, your comments can help indicate what we need to continue doing to keep you happy; if you are unhappy with what you see going on, they can be used to make changes. But, if your voice isn't heard, you can't be part of the solution. Phase two gives you a real opportunity to create a more idealized work environment. I am not just asking to hear the voices of department heads. I want to hear everyone's opinions—executives, assistants, associates, and staff. During phase two, everyone's opinion carries equal weight. We cannot correct problems we don't know about. I cannot urge you enough to speak out. Please, take advantage of your power.

After we have merged and identified our strengths and weaknesses, we will be ready to move onto phase three, the modification stage. This is the point in our process where we will put your feedback into action. After the corporate department receives your input and analyzes it, we will work on the necessary retooling and revamping to take our company into the twenty-first century.

In summation, what may seem like a dark time of uncertainty to you right now, actually provides an opportunity, as Roethke observed, to see more clearly than ever. Open your eyes. Take notice. Make suggestions. Help us to notice, to identify, and to modify. And if you do, I promise you that you'll find the future looking brighter than ever.

New Business Pitch

It's Generation Y versus the Baby Boomers! Look in the advertising and marketing trade papers, and that's all you'll read about. Or just look around you; it seems as if every ad campaign these days is aimed at today's hip youth culture, or at more affluent urban professionals. That's because after spending millions on marketing studies and focus groups, businesses everywhere have decided that targeting one of these two lucrative markets will yield them the highest sales. It's impossible to target everyone, and a specialized ad campaign aimed at a very clearly defined audience is the way to go. Or so the conventional thinking would indicate.

As you've announced your decision to switch ad agencies, I'm betting more than one agency has come to you proclaiming its success in advertising to one of those two core markets. I'm here, though, to tell you it doesn't need to be an either/or situation. What if you could target Generation Y *and* the Baby Boomers? And what if you could do it without having to spend more on your advertising budget? Wouldn't your sales then be twice as high?

What the Devon Agency can offer you that you'll find nowhere else is a creative staff that knows both today's youth culture and the baby boomer generation inside and out. That's because we've structured our company in a way that uniquely combines younger and more mature sensibilities. Our creative department consists of several teams, each one pairing older, more experienced art directors and copywriters who have been selling to the Boomer market for the past ten years with younger talents who bring their fresh perspectives and knowledge of today's youth market. We don't play to one market or the other; we play to both. And we're able to do it because our staff comes from both those core demographic groups.

Let me show you some of our exciting work. [SHOW SERIES OF SLIDES OF MAGAZINE ADS.] This is a series of magazine ads we created for Fashion Attic. You can see how we drew upon a range of today's hottest up-and-coming young start, and paired them up with the Oscar winning actors and actresses who are the kings and queens of Hollywood's old guard. Now let me show you how we expanded on that campaign in our television spots. [SHOW REEL OF COMMERCIAL CLIPS.] Our account executives were careful to place these ads in a range of media outlets, from TV shows popular with the twenty-one and under set, to more affluent, business-oriented publications.

What did this new campaign mean for Fashion Attic? I'll show you. [PUT CHART ON EASEL.] This chart documents Fashion Attic's sales before and after our campaign. You can see that after the initial launch in the magazines, sales rose 22 percent. And after the commercial spots started running, they rose another staggering 15 percent.

How would you like to see that same kind of increase in sales here at Close Clothes? You've done a remarkable job of making your Casual Khaki pants a fashion staple of the affluent twenty-five to forty-year-old set. But why stop there? Why not target those teenagers and college kids? The right campaign, aimed at a broader market, could double your potential sales.

Our work for Fashion Attic that I just showed you has proven what many claim to be impossible: it *is* possible to market to Generation Y *and* the Baby Boomers with one campaign. It's possible, but how many agencies are doing it? How many agencies *can* do it? Only the Devon Agency has the kind of diverse mixture of talents—and daring imagination—to make these campaigns work. Let the Devon Agency put those talents to work for you.

Presenting an Award

One of the most rewarding components of my job is getting to reward others. And no award gives me greater pleasure to bestow than Employee of the Month. Often the only reward for hard work is the quiet satisfaction of seeing a job well done. And while this pride is meaningful, it is important to the company that we take time to shine a spotlight on individual players on our team.

As you know, since we began awarding an Employee of the Month back in June 1995, we have often lauded employees whose contributions are obvious, such as winning a new client or creating a new campaign. It's important, though, that we take equal pride in those workers whose skillful and steadfast work is an integral part of this company's overall success. For this month's award, the awards committee and myself decided to reward just such a devoted worker—and we knew almost immediately who was most deserving of it. It is with great pride that I bestow this month's Employee of the Month award to Christopher Paceyak.

Christopher is the embodiment of a true company man. His dedication to this company comes through in his every action, from the extra hours he often devotes to his job to his enthusiastic coaching of our softball team. His can-do attitude has been the driving force behind many an outstanding project, which he oversees from start to finish with an eye on perfection. His quiet confidence in times of crisis frequently has a calming effect on even his most stressed-out coworkers, and his morale and good humor have proven downright infectious. Christopher knows that in order for him to look good at his job, it behooves him to have the whole department look good. His colleagues have marveled at how he always knows when someone needs a helping hand and then doesn't bat an eye about offering his services.

In today's often impersonal work world, Christopher always makes sure he is accessible. Our clients often ask for him by name, and his friendly attitude never fails in setting them at ease. I'll never forget the time I went to pitch a new client—the Allenberg Theatre—and at the start of our meeting, they asked me if Christopher Paceyak would be available to work on their account! They'd heard about his wonderful work through our other clients.

Woody Allen once remarked that 80 percent of success is showing up. Christopher has shown that not to be true. It's not just showing up that makes him such an inspiration—although he has maintained a stellar attendance record throughout his employment here—it's the warmth, dedication, and energy he brings with him into this office each and every day that have made all of us a little bit happier to be here. Christopher, it is with great delight that I present you with December's Employee of the Month plaque. We here at Ticketflash would also like to give you a gift certificate for a dinner for four at your favorite local restaurant. Enjoy. Thank you for your devotion. And, Christopher, keep up the great work.

Receiving an Award

Sophocles once said, "Look and you will find it—what is unsought will go undetected." It was this philosophy that led me to this company. When I graduated from college ten years ago, I had a definite image in mind of the kind of place where I wanted to work, and I set out to find it. I was looking for a company with the potential to grow, and that I could grow with. I was looking for a nurturing boss who could teach me through example and experience. I was looking for coworkers I could depend on and also consider friends. I was looking for an environment where I could feel free to think creatively and, best of all possible worlds, even be rewarded for it. I knew it was a tall order, but I was determined that if such a company existed, I would find it. I even turned down a few offers because they just didn't seem right. But when I stepped through the doors at Ticketflash, it did seem to have it all. Ten years later, I'm happy to say that initial search yielded exactly what I'd been seeking—and more.

I don't know many people who are still excited, ten years down the line, to get out of bed to go to work. But I am. And to receive an award for something I love doing is a true gift for which I am grateful.

When I found out that I was being given this award, it gave me time to reflect on the period of time I have spent at Ticketflash. I will never forget the first major account I ran, the Second Avenue Theater. The theater director was a real character, and I worked day and night trying to please him. As our first season working with them came to a close, I went out with some coworkers to celebrate making it through without a major mishap. Wouldn't you know, though, that I got a call from the director that very night? It seemed that a batch of tickets we'd ordered for them had been printed entirely in purple.

Well, I thought he was going to flip his lid. I also thought that would put a fast end to my employment here. But I got the surprise of my life when he then told me how he always hated the old tickets and that purple was his favorite color. So I learned a valuable lesson. Success has a lot to do with hard work, time, and effort, but sometimes luck plays a part in it too. And I've been very lucky.

I've been lucky to work with such incredible people whom I admire and love. Marlon, thank you for the gracious and moving presentation. This is overwhelming. I have worked under you for my entire tenure here. I have learned immeasurable business savvy from you. In my estimation, this award is as much yours as it is mine. I would not be accepting an award of excellence without the wisdom and confidence you have imparted to me. Thank you.

Josh, Katherine, and Kyle, you are the working definition of a dream team. Many people might not think of marketing as a creative field. But with our group, I feel like the Beatles must have felt when they would create a hit song. All elements come together in perfect harmony. And, Josh, I'm not even going to mention the fact that you led the company softball team to the league championships two years in a row! I truly couldn't dream of three more upstanding and fine people I would rather spend such a large chunk of my life with. Thank you. Thank you. Thank you.

I've also been lucky, throughout the years, to have so many wonderful clients whom I've been honored to work with, many of whom, I'm touched to see, are here tonight. Clients with whom I feel so very proud to be associated. Clients I am glad to call friends.

I want to wrap up by once again thanking everyone for giving me this beautiful night, this wonderful award. Your caring guidance, your warm camaraderie, your business! Thank you for giving me a glorious memory of a very proud and happy time in my life, a memory I am sure to reflect upon for years to come. I am truly honored to receive your award of excellence.

Honoring a Retiring Employee

Somerset Maugham once said, "It's a funny thing about life; if you refuse to accept anything but the best, you very often get it." As the head of this company, I have tried to live by this motto, always expecting the best from myself and from everyone who works here. Over the years, some have not seen the value of this thinking and left. Others did value it and left anyway. And then there's Charlie Ryan, who stayed. Charlie stayed for thirty-five years! And each and every day he's been here, he's not only strived to do his best, but inspired everyone around him, myself included, to do so as well.

Charlie, nobody deserves to take it easy more than you do. In your thirty-five years here, you have put so much into this company that it's impossible to imagine what it would have been like had you never walked through our doors. And now, it's impossible to imagine Clearview Industries without your commitment, your energy, your passion. I have never lost a night's sleep over the fate of this company knowing you were around. Charlie, you have been a rock for me and for all of us.

You've been a shining example to so many people here. So many people approached me this week to share a story about you and talk about how much they will miss you. As a tribute to you, I'd like to single a few of them out and share with all of you what they told me about how much Charlie has meant to them.

First, I'd like to ask Brad Green to stand up. Brad came to Clearview fresh from Indiana University. His only practical work experience was a part-time cold call sales job for Mertin Lyle. Charlie, you took Brad under your wing and taught him how to sell. You shared your own work ethic and experience with him, telling him stories of the good old days. And Brad tells me that you made him lists of books to read—philosophy books, business books, even a book of poetry—books that you told Brad give a business executive his back-bone. You took Brad to your business meetings. Introduced him to your clients. Treated him with respect. Treated him as an equal. You gave Brad the room to make mistakes, room to have triumphs. Charlie, you gave Brad the tools that helped him earn this company over two million dollars last year.

Another person whose life has been forever altered for having known you is Dolores Klein. Dolores, please stand up. Dolores has done everything from photocopying and faxing Charlie's documents to giving a speech for Charlie when he had laryngitis! Needless to say, the two of them have been quite a team for over twenty years. When Dolores' dear husband Alex passed away eight years ago with no life insurance, Charlie did more than pay a condolence call. Charlie established a trust fund for Dolores' daughter Shelley. Shelley is now in her third year at Fordham University. Shelley is the first person to go to college in Dolores' family, and she will always have you to thank for such a generous and selfless gift.

I know Brad and Dolores are going to miss you, Charlie. We all are. You better not get so good at golf that you don't let me beat you at least every once in a while! I know that you and Susan are excited to move into your condo in Arizona. I know you are excited to be close to your five beautiful grandchildren. I know that you are excited to write that great American novel you are always going on about. I know you are excited to start this new phase of your life.

I am excited for you. But, Charlie, I just want you to know that this company will never be the same without you. I believe I will miss you and think of you every day I continue to run this place. Thank you, Charlie. Thank you for your service. Thank you for being such an inspiration. And, Charlie, thank you for being a friend. Charlie, all of us here wish you all the health, love, and happiness you so much deserve.

Address to Stockholders

We all know that stockholder's meetings can be dreadfully dull. But you can breathe easy. That's not going to be the case here. As we begin our first stockholder meeting here at Flowers Plus, I'm going to set a precedent and start a new yearly tradition. The precedent is that our meeting will be brief and to the point—providing you with all the information you need to know clearly, quickly, and efficiently. And the tradition? I'll get to that later.

Without further adieu, let's look at the facts. If you will consult the handouts we have prepared for you and turn to page three, you will see that in our first quarter, Flowers Plus had a 17 percent increase in profits. As this is our maiden voyage, we are thrilled with this progress. The second quarter projections look even rosier. Okay, I promise, no more flower puns!

We plan to reinvest our profits from quarter one, but we need to decide where and how. Our market research indicates that the money might best be invested into our Internet division. Our Internet division netted the company over $100,000 in its first quarter, and the World Wide Web shows no signs of slowing down. There is huge growth potential here. After much analysis, we believe that our sales will increase directly in proportion to our investments in this area. But we need to take a vote on this matter. Once you have reviewed the collateral material we have provided you with, please fill out the ballot at the back of the packet indicating your support of or opposition to this reinvestment.

Last on our agenda today is a review of Flowers Plus's retail division. Our retail stores are covering their own costs and should start to pull a profit starting next quarter. However, our flower stands made a profit right out of the gate. We propose to take the profits from the stands and use them for in-store promotions at our retail outlets. As you already know, Flowers Plus has primarily marketed itself with a strong commitment to teaching the consumer to have a green thumb. We can expand on this image by giving in-store seminars. This is a relatively inexpensive way to create goodwill and generate new business and hopefully even media buzz all at once. You'll find a detailed proposal in your packet regarding this exciting possibility. You can review it and we'll open it up to discussion at our next quarterly meeting.

To sum up: In our first quarter, we have made more of a profit than our projections indicated. We now want to reinvest in our Internet division and need your vote. And we want to take the excess profits from our stands and funnel the money into retail promotions.

Now, for starting that tradition that I referred to earlier. We'd like to invite you back to our corporate garden where we are going to plant flowers. We hope to end every stockholder's meeting with this activity. To us, it's a symbol of how working together, we can all take a part in the growth of our company.

Analyzing a Problem/Proposing a Solution

Albert Einstein once said, "In the middle of difficulty lies opportunity." And right now, the Plunkett Corporation has its difficulty, namely our sharp decline in sales. But rather than becoming panicked by this downturn, I'd like to take Mr. Einstein's advice. After all, he was a pretty smart man. And I am confident that we do have an opportunity here. Not only can we solve our problems and reverse this decline, but in so doing, we can also make changes that will eventually raise our profits higher than ever. I'll tell you exactly how we can do that in a moment.

But before I can share with you my program for combating our problems, it's important that you first understand them. As you know, I have hired an independent consulting firm to come in and help us analyze this situation. After a three-week period in which they've interviewed and observed us carefully, they have identified three major factors behind Plunkett Corporation's drop in sales that I want to now share with you.

One, we are losing our retailers. Several key retailers have stopped ordering from us entirely, and those that we still have dealings with have been ordering from us far less frequently. Speaking with representatives from these retailers, our consultants heard complaints about the lack of personal contact they receive from us and what they perceive as a decline in service. Our retailers have become frustrated with dealing with our sales reps via telephone and fax, and complain of the difficulty they've had getting responses to their questions and problems. As a result, many of them have turned to other companies with better service.

Two, we are losing consumers. At one time, our marketing and advertising worked for us, but it has become terribly outdated. We've typically geared ourselves to the twenty- to thirty-year-old demographic group. But as they've aged, they've stopped using our products, and we've failed to create new marketing and advertising to appeal to today's youth market. Simply put, we're no longer reaching the people we need to.

And three, we are losing money, money that we shouldn't be losing. The consulting team has prepared a listing of all of our unnecessary expenditures that I am now making available to you. Individual items on this list cost as little as pennies and nickels a day, which is why we often don't give them serious consideration. But when added together, they cost us an astonishing $100,000 in unnecessary spending each month!

So, thanks to our consultants, we now know the three factors behind our declining sales: losing our retailers through poor service, our consumers through outdated marketing and advertising, and our money through wasteful and unnecessary expenditures. That's the bad news. The good news is that having identified the problems we have now come up with solutions.

First, based on the listing of expenditures provided by our consultants, I am trimming the fat here, effective immediately. I am passing out to each of you the new, far more modest monthly budgets for each department. By cutting those pennies and nickels spent each day on the unnecessaries you'll find you still have plenty of money for your operating costs.

Second, I am going to take the money cut from those budgets to help us foster better relations with our retailers and customers. To begin with, I am authorizing more on-site sales visits within the tri-state area. Within the week, I want every member of the sales staff to create a sales call itinerary for themselves and submit it to me. I am also instituting a new bonus system; for each client who you get and hold onto for the year, you'll receive an additional $500 at year's end. Do what you need to keep those clients and keep them happy.

Third, I want us to work closely with marketing to revamp and add to our marketing materials. For one thing, we need to present the most up-to-date sales brochures as possible. Perception is everything and we need to appear as current as we actually are. We cannot afford to look out of date. Technology is moving so fast that what was current even months ago is now obsolete. We need to stay on top of the trends. I'm also hiring a new advertising agency and increasing our advertising budget. We're going to create new, more aggressive campaigns and target them to a broader market.

This is the program I've developed along with our consultants. But I can only put the initial steps in place; you're the ones who have got to make them work. If you succeed, though—and I am certain you will—not only will this time of difficulty be at an end, but we just might be entering a time of our greatest prosperity, and we'll all be able to take part in the benefits. When next we meet, rather than looking at our failures and difficulties, let's be in a position to celebrate our profits and triumphs.

Dedicating a New Facility

St. Bart's Hospital is a Mayfield institution. It has been in existence for over seventy years, and as our community has grown, so has this important facility. The babies born in Mayfield are born at St. Bart's, and the lives saved in Mayfield are saved at St. Bart's. Another Mayfield institution is the Sylvester family. For three generations this family has been a very important part of this community. From Jim Sylvester's service as the high school principal to Lucy Sylvester's successful tenure as our mayor, this family has given so much to their hometown.

Five years ago, the St. Bart's development office received a mixed blessing. We were saddened by the passing of beloved Agnes Sylvester, the matriarch of the Sylvester family. Yet we were surprised and very grateful to learn that in her will, Mrs. Sylvester donated two hundred thousand dollars to St. Bart's to break ground on a new children's wing.

Caring for children was an issue near and dear to Mrs. Sylvester's heart, as it is to the staff at St. Bart's. That is why today we are proud to have the surviving members of the Sylvester family on hand for the groundbreaking and ribbon-cutting ceremony for the new Agnes Sylvester Wing for Children at the St. Bart's Hospital. Children represent our future. As we remember the passing of Agnes Sylvester, let us take comfort in the thought of the many children who will be cared for and even saved at this new facility. In this way, her memory will truly live on.

And now, without further ado, I invite Agnes Sylvester's eldest son, Lee, to please cut the ribbon so that construction may begin on what will be his family's newest contribution to Mayfield.

Giving a Demonstration

I have in my hand a stack of phone message pads. And I'm now going to throw them in the trash. Because with our new voicemail system, they're no longer necessary. Yes, I know you're all a little concerned about having to learn how to use this new voicemail system. But consider this. The days of writing out messages by hand—and all the tedium and miscommunication that went with it—are now over and done with. I can honestly say that within a week, you will be operating the Vspeak 2000 like old pros—and you'll see just how much better this system is than the old way. It's also not nearly as hard to use as you might think. I'm going to take you step by step through the new system. Feel free to take notes if you like, although I will also be providing you with an operations manual that describes everything I'll be showing you. We'll be looking at the three most important facets of this new system: First we are going to discuss call transfers; we will then move onto the voicemail set up; and finally, voicemail retrieval.

Let's start with call transferring. Suppose I answer a call that is actually for Larry Wilkes and I need to transfer it to him. You'll see on these charts that I've distributed that you have all been assigned extension numbers. So when I get the call, I just need to check the extension chart and see that Larry's extension is 220. To transfer this call to him, I first hit the transfer button [SHOW BUTTON ON SAMPLE PHONE], located at the bottom right hand corner of the phone unit. Next, I dial Larry's extension and then I hang up. Let me show you. [DEMONSTRATE TRANSFER.] It's that simple.

I do not, I repeat, I do not hit the hold button during this transfer. It's a common urge that people have to put someone on hold before they transfer a call. If you do hit the hold button, the call will not transfer. But don't worry if you make a mistake and hit the hold button anyway. The worst thing that would happen is that your caller will sit on hold for a minute and then your line will ring again. It's very easy. All you need to remember to transfer a call is transfer-extension-transfer.

Let's say Larry Wilkes is not at his desk or he's on another line and can't get off to answer the other ringing line. The call will then go into voicemail. After five rings, the Vspeak 2000 automatically puts a call into voicemail. What the caller will hear first is a generic greeting. Let's try calling Larry's line right now and hear it. [DEMONSTRATE CALL ON SPEAKERPHONE.] What you just heard was the generic greeting already programmed into the system. Now, if this message is satisfactory to you, you can simply leave it on your phone. However, many people choose to personalize their outgoing voicemail message. Larry, why don't you come up here and I will guide you through recording your own personal voicemail message? Everyone else can do this when they go back to their own desks at the end of the demonstration. [WAIT FOR LARRY TO COME UP.]

All right, Larry. You can either compose your own message, or use the standard script we've provided. You are about to be recorded; are you nervous Larry? Take a deep breath and don't worry about it. You can record your message as many times as you want until you are satisfied. First hit the feature button and then 435. You will then be prompted through the process. I'll put it on speakerphone for you all to hear. You can also follow the instructions in your instruction manual. [HAVE LARRY RECORD HIS MESSAGE/EVERYONE LISTENS ON SPEAKERPHONE.] Okay, now that the message is recorded, you just need to hit feature *** to save it. So, to review: to record a personalized voicemail message, hit feature 435, follow the recorded instructions, and then to save your greeting, hit feature ***.

You can rerecord your personalized messages whenever you like. For example, if you are going away on vacation, you can rerecord your message to tell your callers that you will be out of the office for a week and to dial your assistant's extension for help. Or you can give an alternative phone number at which you can be reached.

The final process I want to review with you today is voicemail retrieval. There are two ways that you can retrieve voicemail. One way is internally, the other is externally. Internally means that you retrieve your messages from somewhere in your office. If you are sitting at your own extension, for example, you can simply hit the voicemail button and punch in your code, and your messages will then play back. Everyone has a code that must be entered to get messages off voicemail, so you don't have to worry about anyone hearing something meant only for you. To receive your secret code, hit feature 456 and let the prompt guide you. If you are at another extension in the office, you simply hit feature 999 and you will be prompted to enter your extension and then your code and then you can receive your messages. Larry, why don't you retrieve messages from my voicemail? [DEMONSTRATE RETRIEVAL OF MESSAGES FROM VOICEMAIL.]

Finally, if you are calling from outside the office, you can dial the main number and ask the receptionist to put you through to your own extension. Once connected to your extension, hit feature 227 and you will be prompted to give your password or code and then you can retrieve your messages. If you are calling during nonbusiness hours, you will be placed into the general voicemail mailbox. You then hit the # key and then feature 724. The prompt will then ask you for your extension. After you punch in your extension, hit the # key again. This will take you to the prompt that asks for your personal code. And that's it; you can retrieve your messages.

I don't want to overload you with too much information today. So, why doesn't everybody go back to his or her desk and record messages. I will be back next week to go through some more features of the Vspeak 2000. I guarantee that by then, you'll be telling me you don't know what you did without voicemail for so long.

Running a Meeting

We've all heard the saying that "talk is cheap." I'm not so certain I agree with that. One thing I've seen in our monthly staff meetings is just how valuable talking can be. The discussions we've had here have led to important policy changes that have resulted in a number of noticeable improvements in this company. So I firmly believe that talk is definitely not cheap; in fact, I think it is crucial to our continued success.

However, I have been thinking about another factor that is perhaps even more valuable than talking, a skill that we've unfortunately overlooked too often. And that's listening. All of us here are quite skilled orators. We know how to make our points clearly, convincingly, and eloquently. But how many of us are skilled listeners? More and more I'm convinced that active listening—making a concentrated effort to really listen to one another—is the only way we can get an accurate picture of what's happening in this company. It's also the best way for us all to work toward solving problems and to generate great new ideas.

So I've decided to make listening the focus of today's meeting; as I see it, listening, in some way or other, informs our agenda today in three important ways.

First, I've personally been doing a great deal of listening myself lately. I've spent the last two weeks visiting each and every department in our company, making it my main goal to listen to what our employees have to say. Based on what I heard, I have identified four issues that appear to be most in need of immediate consideration: one, the new computer system; two, the overtime hours issue; three, the development of the company Web site; and four, the loss of the D&R account.

Second, I want you to listen to each other in today's meeting as carefully as I have listened to all of you in the past two weeks. To that end, I have asked each department head to prepare a brief report that touches on the issues I just listed. While each department head reads that report today, make it your sole aim to listen. Really listen. Don't take notes. Don't make comments. Don't even ask questions. Just listen.

Third, when each department head is finished speaking, when we've all listened to what he or she has to say, then there will be time for talk. We can open the floor for questions and for open discussion. However, again, I'd ask that you all concentrate on those listening skills. Rather than just making a comment, or offering an opinion, listen to what the person before you has said. See if you can build on that topic and somehow incorporate it into your own statement. This will insure that we're all actively listening to one another.

I think we'll find these efforts at active listening make the meeting much more productive. Feel free, afterwards, to let me know what you think. I can guarantee, I'll listen to whatever you have to say.

Now, time for us to listen to our first speaker: Carol Jacobson from Financing. Go ahead, Carol, the floor is yours . . .

Giving a Wedding Toast

When David asked me to be his best man, I have to admit I felt nervous at the thought of giving this toast. It made me nervous because I realized I'd have to somehow pick from the thousands of embarrassing stories involving David's bizarre dating experiences that I know. I thought I might tell you about the time he managed to break his nose while out on a blind date. I also thought I could tell you about the date who managed to steal David's wallet during their romantic dinner. But then I figured, no. It's his wedding, so I'll give the guy a break. Instead of embarrassing him, I'll tell a story about myself. It just so happens to be the story of how I met Lisa, now Mrs. David Bernstein, for the first time.

I'd been hearing David describe this fantastic new woman in his life for weeks. Based on everything he told me about Lisa and her background, I had a picture of her in my mind as being pretty high class and stylish, on par with say Grace Kelly or Audrey Hepburn. So you can imagine how panicked I was when, one Saturday night, minutes after I'd come in from a run, David buzzed my apartment to tell me that he and Lisa were downstairs and wanted to come up.

I had been working all week on a nightmarish project that kept me at the office until late hours. To call my apartment a sty at that point is probably an insult to pigs. And this was the time David chose to introduce me to his Grace Kelly. So I did what any guy in my position would do—I tried to hide the mess; you know, frantically shoving the pizza boxes under the couch, putting dirty dishes back in cabinets, stuff like that. I didn't have time, though, to change out of my sweaty workout clothes I was still wearing after my run.

Well, David and Lisa come in, and of course Lisa couldn't be any nicer. After kissing me hello, she went to the fridge, helped herself to a beer, and threw herself down on the couch to relax. Within about five minutes, after we'd compared notes about our favorite TV shows and movies, I felt like I'd known her as long as I did David. And I've only felt even closer to her ever since.

As many of you probably know, when your best friend gets married, it can be a wonderful, happy occasion. But I also hope you know, like I do, the special joy you get when your best friend marries someone you can consider a friend. And so, I'd like you all to lift up your glasses to toast the happy couple with me.

To David and Lisa, may your love, like your wedding rings, be without end. And may all of us be there to share in the joy it brings you.

Welcome to Company Outing

Ever since I saw the movie *The Shining*, I've been pretty sensitive to the dangers of overwork. You probably know the scene I'm thinking of. Shelley Duvall comes to check up on her husband Jack Nicholson's progress on the novel he's been slaving away at, and finds he's written over and over, "All work and no play makes Jack a dull boy." That's right before he goes bonkers and tries to kill her with an axe. Since I've lately been detecting that same "Jack-like" glint in some of your eyes, especially the folks over in marketing, I think our company outing couldn't come at a better time.

All kidding aside, we've all been working incredibly hard the past few months. Taking on that massive D&R account meant our workload increased by more than 30 percent. For most of you, it meant long hours. It meant late nights. And it meant plenty of stress. But everyone at Jones & Robertson rose to the challenge. And as a result of all that extra effort, I'm proud to announce that we had our most successful quarter ever.

And that's something worth celebrating with a day off. So we've rented this fabulous club for your exclusive use for the entire day. I hope you'll find something to do you enjoy. Play tennis or golf, take a dip in the pool, or enjoy a steam in the sauna. Later on, we'll have a terrific barbecue out on the lake. Just one thing: you are officially forbidden to discuss anything at all having to do with D&R, the office, or work! Talking about work can make Jack a dull boy too! Today is about fun. Today is about rest and relaxation. You've had your weeks of "all work," now it's time to play.

Press Conference Announcement

Thank you all for coming on such short notice. Those of you who don't know me, I'm Jacqueline Bruckner, vice president of public relations for Netsurf Enterprises. Beside me is William Berg, head of press relations for Global Entertainment. First I'll read a brief statement, and then both Mr. Berg and myself will be available to answer questions.

After six months of negotiation talks, the boards of directors of Netsurf and Global Entertainment have finalized arrangements for a merger between the two companies to go into effect on January 1 of next year. The new company will be called Global Netsurf, and the merger will make it the largest new media production company in existence. Bringing together the technology developed by Netsurf with the resources of Global Entertainment, Global Netsurf will be able to provide computer users with an unprecedented number of entertainment resources made available exclusively over the Internet.

Laura Smith, former president of Netsurf, will serve as the CEO of the new company. Roger Atkins, former head of Global Entertainment, will serve as president of production. The corporate headquarters of Global Netsurf will remain in New York, while the product development and production facilities will move to a new location to be determined. At this time, there are no plans to layoff any employees from either company.

Now, Mr. Berg and myself are happy to take your questions. I should first explain, though, that at this time, we are only authorized to answer questions having to do with the structure of and future agenda for the new company, and how the merger will affect consumers, employees, and stockholders. We cannot at this time disclose any specific terms of the merger agreement. However, Ms. Smith and Mr. Atkins will both be available to answer questions at a future press conference.

Welcoming a New Employee

My grandmother, who is without a doubt the wisest person I know, has a simple yet tremendously insightful philosophy about cooking. She says, when it comes to cooking, "if you put in good, you get good." And she's right. She always prepares meals using the freshest, tastiest, most high quality ingredients; and by putting those fine ingredients into her cooking, whatever she makes always comes out superb.

As the director of human resources for Aztec, Inc., I've found myself using my grandmother's philosophy as a guidepost for hiring all new employees. Like my grandmother and her faith in good ingredients, I've believed that, by "putting good" into this company, "good" will result. So I've made a commitment to seeking out only the best, most accomplished and skilled people to come be a part of Aztec, Inc. And the results of those hiring practices are evident in this company's outstanding achievements that only seem to increase with each talented new person who joins us.

Today, we welcome a new ingredient to our extraordinary company mix, someone who has already proven herself to be a genius at what she does. Andrea Gold, who joins us today as a vice president of marketing, comes to us from Zip Four Communications, where she worked in the marketing department for the past eight years. In addition to working on an impressive list of high-profile accounts that includes Cryon Comm, Bengal, and Genie.com, Andrea was the genius behind the "Synergy" campaign, which set new industry standards in computer marketing strategies. That campaign also earned Andrea the 2005 "Marketing Mind" of the Year Award from the American Association of Communications and Marketing Professionals.

Yes, there's no question that, in the world of marketing, Andrea is one of the best there is working today, and we are very lucky to have her. I'm certain that she'll be "putting good" into our company, and we'll all benefit from her contribution in the days to come. I hope in the next few days, you'll take the time to introduce yourselves to Andrea and to make her feel welcome. Help her to blend in and become a part of this special, talented mix we are so fortunate to have here at Aztec.

Farewell to a Departing Employee

Marcus Aurelius Antoninus, the Roman emperor and philosopher, once offered these wise words: "Loss is nothing else but change, and change is Nature's delight." In thinking about how I might offer a fond farewell to Susan Atkinson, I had cause to think about those words. While we are sad to lose Susan, her departure from here is certain to be the delight, if not of Nature Herself, then certainly of all who are fortunate to work with her in the future.

Susan first came to Lerner, Lerner and Kaye in 1990, as a first year associate who had just graduated with distinction from New York University Law School. We knew she was special right from day one, when she was thrust into the morass of the Ryan vs. Ryan case, and proved herself much more than capable; her long hours, her careful research, and her instrumental input all played an important part in our success with that case. On all of the cases that Susan became involved with since then, she continued to impress all of the partners and senior associates with whom she worked.

I know that Bob Abrams, who served as Susan's mentor, will particularly miss her. But Bob also told me that Susan has learned all he has to teach her, and that it is indeed the time for her to move on to bigger and better things. When Susan was offered an opportunity to come in as a partner at Weiss Weinberg, he encouraged her to take it with his blessing.

And so it is that we will have to say farewell to Susan. Susan, we thank you for all that you have done for us over the years. We thank you for your hard work. We thank you for being a friendly colleague and co-worker, whose warmth and good humor have continually brightened the halls of this office. We will sorely miss you, but we wish you the best of luck in your new position.

Loss, as Emperor Antoninus commented, is really just a form of change, and change can and often does present an opportunity for all involved. While we are saddened to lose Susan, we can also look forward to welcoming new faces, and whatever unique experiences those individuals bring with them. We hope they will prove as smart, resourceful, and enthusiastic as Susan has been.

Paying Tribute to an Honoree

They say that actions speak more than words. It only follows that if you want to judge a man's character, you look at more than what he says; you look at what he does. Dr. Mark Allen knew that to make a new pediatrics intensive care facility a reality, it would take more than words, so he personally took action. He knew that sitting around complaining about the hospital's lack of resources, or repeatedly making demands of the board of directors would not be enough to bring that new facility to fruition. So, he personally raised the funds to make it happen. Today, we honor Dr. Mark Allen for those tireless efforts. But we also pay tribute to him for much more. We pay tribute to the fine doctor, colleague, and friend he has shown himself to be time and time again, through his words and his actions.

Do you want to know what kind of a person Mark Allen is? I'll tell you a story that will show you what kind of a person he is. When I was a young pediatrics intern at this hospital many years ago, Dr. Allen was the first resident I was assigned to. On my very first day of work, I had a fender-bender on the way to the hospital and, as a result, showed up more than thirty minutes late. Having heard all kinds of nightmarish stories about how the residents could come down on the interns for the slightest of infractions, I came to the hospital prepared to be seriously chewed out. Instead, Dr. Allen, hearing about the accident, expressed genuine concern about how I was. Then he called his mechanic and arranged to have my car picked up and repaired. But he did more than that. At the end of the shift, he drove me home. And he picked me up the next day, and drove me home the next night. He drove me back and forth to work every day until my car was fixed.

Now that I've gotten to know him much better, I realize that his kind treatment of me that day is typical of his interactions with all the doctors, nurses, and patients in this hospital. I learned that day that Dr. Mark Allen is that rare kind of doctor who, in an age when doctors are too often stereotyped as cold, self-involved automatons, genuinely likes working with other people and, without making a big deal of it, without having to be asked, will often go out of his way to do a favor for someone or help them out when they're in need.

You want to know what kind of a doctor Mark Allen is? Ask the nurses who work here. They'll tell you, as they told me when I asked them that question earlier this week, that he's the kind of doctor who not only knows them all by name, but always remembers their birthdays with a card and flowers.

What kind of a doctor is Mark Allen? Ask his patients. They'll tell you he's the kind of doctor who expresses sincere interest in who they are, taking the time to chat about their likes and hobbies, to talk about the latest popular movie or TV show. One patient told me that Dr. Allen, after learning that her favorite author is Charles Dickens, brought her his copy of *Great Expectations* to read while she was recovering from surgery. He's also the kind of doctor, his patients tell me, who always treats them with compassion and dignity, answering their questions and concerns with the utmost consideration and respect.

What kind of doctor is Mark Allen? Ask his colleagues, the other doctors who work in this hospital. They'll tell you he's the kind of doctor they admire, the one who sets a standard for a certain kind of conscientious patient care they strive to match. I know that's certainly been the case with myself. I can say with utmost confidence that I wouldn't be the doctor I am today were it not for his fine example that I have made it my personal goal to emulate.

Talk to his colleagues, the nurses, and his patients, and they'll tell you what kind of doctor Mark Allen is. But if you want to see what kind of person he is, look at his actions and what those actions have achieved—a glorious new facility that is helping save hundreds of children's lives. For achieving that, for being a man of action, we pay tribute today, just as we honor him for being the caring, compassionate, and inspiring figure who we have the great privilege of working with each day.

Introducing a Guest Speaker

I have the great pleasure today of introducing you to someone who, in addition to being my favorite writer, I am fortunate to consider a mentor and a close friend. As it happens, Quentin James was also the first acquaintance I made when I began teaching at Columbia in 1992. I had just been hired as an instructor in the creative writing program, and had been in my new office for about ten minutes, when Quentin walked in. I of course knew who he was; the man, after all, had just won the Pulitzer Prize for *Dogcatcher*. But he introduced himself anyway, and then, to my surprise and my delight, sat in the chair opposite my desk, and proceeded to engage me in conversation. I just couldn't believe that this famous author, who I personally considered one of today's greatest novelists, was taking the time to sit and talk with me. I was even more surprised when he proceeded to inform me, after forty-five minutes chatting together, that I was actually sitting in his office! After I turned bright red and finished sputtering my apology, I asked him why he didn't kick me out when he first came in and found me at his desk. And I'll never forget his response. He smiled and said, "Because I like the company."

In retrospect, I realize that I shouldn't have been quite as surprised by that first meeting as I was. Because anyone who reads Quentin James' novels knows that only someone who has that kind of fascination with other people could create the wonderful, absolutely believable characters that he's famous for. I'm thinking of characters like Evelyn, the alcoholic nightclub singer of *Blue Streak*, and Derek, the cop who dreams of a career as a chef in *Walking the Beat*—characters who are such unique, fully drawn individuals that we feel we know them, and who, when we've reached the last page, we find ourselves missing.

During one of our many conversations about writing, I once asked Quentin about the process he uses to create these characters who are not only realistic but also captivating, complicated individuals. And he told me, "It's easy. I just listen to what people have to say about themselves. Anything you need to know about creating characters you can learn from listening to the people you meet."

As far back as high school, Quentin demonstrated that keen interest in listening to what people have to say. Serving as the editor of his school newspaper, the *Gryphon Gazette*, he wrote a weekly column in which he profiled a student or teacher whom he'd interviewed. That column won him an award from the High School Press Association, and led to a summer internship at the *Washington Post*. In college, Quentin continued writing these profiles for the Princeton paper. Acting further on his interest in people, and demonstrating the compassion and empathy that critics today describe as hallmarks of his writing, he began volunteering his time at a peer crisis counseling center.

The experience of listening to his fellow students share their crises and troubles, and reveal in many cases their most intimate emotions and desires, became the inspiration for Quentin's first novel, *Hear Hear*, published by Random House in 1973 to universal acclaim. Arlene Kreig, reviewing the book in the *New York Times*, hailed it as the arrival of an important new talent in American fiction. That impressive debut was followed by five more novels and three short story collections, all of which have earned tremendous critical praise and accolades. Four of those novels have been turned into successful films, the most recent one, *The Last Train of the Night*, earning Quentin an Oscar for his screenplay. That Oscar can take its place alongside Quentin's Pulitzer, and two American Book awards.

Quentin is currently at work on his next novel, tentatively titled, *For Crying Out Loud*. Today, we have the great privilege of having him here to read an excerpt from it in person, as well as talk to us more about his distinctive writing process. Please, join me in welcoming the wonderful writer responsible for creating all of those marvelous characters who we know and love, my friend, colleague, and occasional office mate, Quentin James.

Welcome to Convention/Conference

I'm here to officially welcome you all to the thirty-second annual convention of the American Association of Media Practitioners and Developers. It's entirely appropriate that this year's convention take place over Columbus Day Weekend, when we honor an explorer who bravely set out to explore new worlds. This year's convention, focusing on "Cutting Edge Developments in New Media," offers all of us the opportunity to explore exciting new terrain. I invite all of you to approach this year's events with Columbus's "spirit of discovery" in mind, taking advantage of the many ways in which you too might explore the unfamiliar—and discover a great deal in the process.

First, the various panels that have been organized for the next three days promise exciting revelations for all who attend them. Each panel, which will consist of at least three renowned speakers who are experts in their respective fields, will address a major topic or issue related to New Media, such as "Children's Safety and the Net" and "Synergies: Aligning New Media with Other Entertainment Venues." You might learn more about a topic with which you were already familiar; or you might also find yourself discovering a whole new world of ideas and information you didn't know existed. Either way, you'll have many opportunities to explore fascinating new terrain with these reputable speakers.

Second, the key note address will provide, for all of us, an important window into the world of the future. We are privileged to have as our key note speaker Margaret Anderson, the chair of the Media Studies program at Harvard University and the acclaimed author of the international bestseller *Mediaworld*, who is widely regarded as the world's leading expert in the analysis of the societal effects of media technologies. In her address, titled "Tomorrow and Tomorrow and Tomorrow: The New Media Future," Dr. Anderson will assess the various ways in which current new media technology is shaping the future. That address will take place tomorrow, following lunch, in the Crystal Ballroom.

Third, throughout the conference, you are invited to explore the "New Media Technologies" trade show on the convention floor, where you're likely to make any number of thrilling discoveries. Here, you'll find various demonstrations and samples of the latest Internet products, services, and technologies being developed—including the first "virtual reality" Web site, and an "interactive movie database."

Finally, as you attend these various events, keep in mind that other people can also serve as doorways to new worlds. Hearing of someone else's background and experiences can often make for fascinating discoveries that can educate and profoundly affect us. So take advantage of this rare gathering of hundreds of people working in the same field to meet one another, talk with one another, and learn from one another.

In conclusion, I welcome you once again to our thirty-second annual convention: "Cutting Edge Developments in New Media." Now, to quote another great explorer, it's time for you to "boldly go where no man has gone before, to explore strange new worlds." Enjoy the journey.

Index

Transcendental meditation (TM), 7
Trends, 32
TV comedy, 68
TV interviews, 135, 140–43
Typefaces, 92
Type order, 32

U
Universal themes, 36

V
Verdana, 92
Videoconferencing, 120–21
Videos, 88–89
Virtual meetings, 119–23
Virtual Reference Desk, 26
Visual aids. *See* Audio-visuals
Visual effects, in PowerPoint presentation, 94
Visualization, 16–17
Vivid language, 52–53
Voice
    squeaky, 8
    taking care of your, 5–6

W
Web conferencing, 121–23
Web sites, for professional speakers, 155–56
Wedding toasts, 223–24
Welcome speech, 225, 227–28
Whiteboards, 85–86
Workshops
    brochures for, 172–74
    filling seats at, 175–76
    marketing of, 168–71
    out-of-town facilities for, 174–75
Writer, hiring a, 66–68
Written questions, 76

Y
Yoga, 7–8